CLOSENESS

in Personal and Professional Relationships

A C.G. JUNG FOUNDATION BOOK

The C. G. Jung Foundation for Analytical Psychology is dedicated to helping men and women grow in conscious awareness of the psychological realities in themselves and society, find healing and meaning in their lives and greater depth in their relationships, and live in response to their discovered sense of purpose. It welcomes the public to attend its lectures, seminars, films, symposia, and workshops and offers a wide selection of books for sale through its bookstore. The Foundation also publishes *Quadrant,* a semi-annual journal, and books on Analytical Psychology and related subjects. For information about Foundation programs or membership, please write to the C. G. Jung Foundation, 28 East 39th Street, New York, NY 10016.

CLOSENESS

in Personal and Professional Relationships

EDITED BY

HARRY A. WILMER

SHAMBHALA

Boston & London

1992

Shambhala Publications, Inc.
Horticultural Hall
300 Massachusetts Avenue
Boston, Massachusetts 02115

Shambhala Publications, Inc.
Random Century House
20 Vauxhall Bridge Road
London SW1V 2SA

Library of Congress Cataloging-in-Publication Data
Closeness in personal and professional relationships / edited by Harry
A. Wilmer—1st ed.
p.   cm.
"A C. G. Jung Foundation book."
Includes bibliographical references.
ISBN 0-87773-638-3 (alk. paper)
1. Psychotherapist and patient.   2. Intimacy (Psychology).
3. Psychotherapists—Professional ethics.   4. Interpersonal
relationships.   I. Wilmer, Harry A., 1917–
RC480.8.C56   1992
616.89′14—dc20   91-52523
CIP

"It is always safe to assume that people are more subtle and less sensitive than they seem."

—ERIC HOFFER

Contents

Contents

Foreword

J ohn Donne's statement, "No man is an island" (meaning to say in his sixteenth-century way that nor is any woman or child), has found few people who are willing to argue with its premise. The statement reposes in the mind and leaves the lips with palpable sincerity. Yet, each of us in our daily lives proves John Donne was not only wrong to make such a pronouncement, but naive.

Knowing what we know of the killing nature of loneliness, we should be able to say that a conference on closeness and a book on closeness are redundant expenditures of energy, intelligence, and time. Unfortunately, because of our timidity and rampant ignorance we have to admit that we need the conference (and many more), and we need this book on closeness in the hands of the hopeless, the heartless, and the homeless. Each of us falls under one, if not all, of those categories.

From the first moment of birth when we are forced by nature and mother to exit that safe, warm, nurturing world where we do not even have the responsibility of breathing for ourselves, we begin to long for the impossibility which is total closeness. Each baby born in Beijing, Paris, Texas and France, Jerusalem and Johannesburg, aches to be wrapped round with unconditional closeness. It is interesting that as we accept more completely our separation and aloneness, we deny our need to touch (and be touched), which is singularly unfortunate. But we go further than that. We deny the needs of other human beings to touch and be touched.

I applaud Dr. Harry A. Wilmer and the Institute for the Humanities at Salado. I applaud the men and women who participated in this book on closeness. We, the human race, are in desperate need of men and women who are vulnerable enough to be courageous enough to probe their own vulnerabilities. I am enheartened when I see psychologists, psychiatrists, and social therapists who show their concern for life on our planet by examining themselves and their lives and then revealing the results of their examination.

We are counseled, "Physician heal thyself." I take this to mean that if each of us tries to heal ourselves, the race will respond positively. When the race responds positively, we will find more people holding hands, more people looking into each other's eyes, and more people saying no man nor woman nor child is an island. Each of us is a touching continent on the planet which is human life.

Maya Angelou

About the Contributors

Kendra Crossen is an editor at Shambhala Publications in Boston and a member of the board of directors of Meher Baba Information Center in Cambridge, Massachusetts.

Joseph L. Henderson, M.D., is a Jungian analyst in private practice in San Francisco. After his personal analysis with C. G. Jung, he studied medicine at St. Bartholomew's Hospital medical school in London. His writings include a chapter in Jung's book *Man and His Symbols,* as well as *Thresholds of Initiation, The Wisdom of the Serpent* (co-authored with Maud Oakes), *Cultural Attitudes in Psychological Perspective,* and *Shadow and Self,* a collection of papers on analytical psychology.

Thomas B. Kirsch, M.D., is a Jungian analyst in private practice in Palo Alto, California. He received his medical degree from Yale Medical School and completed psychiatric training at Stanford University. He graduated from and is past president of the C. G. Jung Institute of San Francisco. He currently is president of the International Association for Analytical Psychology. Dr. Kirsch has written numerous articles on dreams and the life and work of C. G. Jung.

Mary Ann Mattoon, Ph.D., a Jungian analyst in private practice in Minneapolis, Minnesota, is a diplomate of the

C. G. Jung Institute, Zurich, and clinical professor of psychology at the University of Minnesota. She received her doctorate in psychology from the University of Minnesota in 1970. Dr. Mattoon is the author of *Understanding Dreams, Jungian Psychology in Perspective,* and articles in Jungian journals. She was the editor of two volumes of proceedings of Congresses of the International Association for Analytical Psychology: *The Archetype of Shadow in a Split World* (1986) and *Personal and Archetypal Dynamics in the Analytical Relationship* (1989).

Diane Wood Middlebrook is the author of *Anne Sexton: A Biography* and the editor, with Diana Hume George, of *The Selected Poems of Anne Sexton.* She is a professor of English at Stanford University, where she has also served as director of the Center for Research on Women.

Carol A. Mouché is Editor of *Environmental Protection* magazine and has been a journalist with newspapers and magazines for twelve years. She was previously Editor for Program Development at the Institute for the Humanities at Salado and Associate Editor of the Institute's book publications. She has won national awards for writing and nature photography. She graduated with a degree in journalism from Southwest Texas State University at San Marcos.

Peter Rutter, M.D., a psychiatrist and Jungian analyst, is a faculty member and former chair of the Ethics Committee of the C. G. Jung Institute of San Francisco. He is a holder of the distinguished teacher award in Health and Medical Sciences at the University of California, Berkeley, where he taught for eight years. He has consulted, lectured, and given workshops on sexual exploitation to psychology and clergy groups in the United States, Canada, and Great Britain. His book, *Sex in the Forbidden Zone,* is also being published in French, German, Italian, Dutch, Finnish, and Portuguese editions.

James Shultz, M.D, is a psychiatrist and Jungian analyst in private practice in Austin, Texas. At the time of writing his contribution to *Closeness,* he was a candidate with the Inter-Regional Society of Jungian Analysts. Dr. Shultz is Clinical Assistant Professor of Psychiatry at the University of Texas Health Sciences Center at San Antonio. He received his doctorate in medicine from the University of Texas Southwestern Medical School, Dallas.

June Singer is a Zurich-trained Jungian analyst and a member of the Jung Institute of San Francisco. She is also a founding member of the Inter-Regional Society of Jungian Analysts and of the Jung Institute of Chicago. Her most recent book is *Seeing through the Visible World*; she is also the author of *Boundaries of the Soul; The Unholy Bible: Jung, Blake, and the Collective Unconscious; Androgyny: The Opposites Within*; and *Energies of Love.* She is in private practice in Palo Alto, California.

Montague Ullman, M.D., is a psychiatrist and psychoanalyst who founded the dream laboratory at the Maimonides Medical Center, Brooklyn, New York. He devotes himself full-time to dream research and the development of group approaches to dreamwork. He is currently clinical professor of psychiatry emeritus at Albert Einstein College of Medicine. Dr. Ullman is the author or coauthor of several books, including *Dream Telepathy* and *Working with Dreams,* and co-editor of *The Variety of Dream Experience* and *Handbook of States of Consciousness.*

Joseph Wakefield, M.D., is a senior training analyst for the Inter-Regional Society of Jungian Analysts and is in private practice in Austin, Texas. He received a medical degree from Stanford Medical School and residency training at Langley Porter Neuropsychiatric Institute, San Francisco. He was trained and certified in Jungian analysis through the C. G. Jung Institute in San Francisco. Dr. Wakefield has an interest in cross-cultural psychiatry in Central America.

Karl E. Weick, Ph.D., Rensis Likert Collegiate Professor of Organizational Behavior and Psychology at the University of Michigan, is the former editor of *Administrative Science Quarterly*. Dr. Weick received his doctorate in psychology from Ohio State University. His writings on such issues as the effects of stress on thinking and imagination, applying social science, and the management of professionals are collected in four books, including *The Social Psychology of Organizing*, and he co-authored *Managerial Behavior, Performance, and Effectiveness*.

Harry A. Wilmer, M.D., Ph.D., is a consulting Jungian analyst in private practice in Salado, Texas. He is founder, president, and director of the Institute for the Humanities at Salado. He has written more than two hundred scientific articles and is the author or editor of eleven books, including *Practical Jung: Nuts and Bolts of Jungian Psychotherapy, Facing Evil, Vietnam in Remission, Mother Father*, and *Creativity: Paradoxes and Reflections*. His book *Social Psychiatry in Action* was made into an Alcoa Premier film called *People Need People*, which aired on ABC and starred Lee Marvin and Arthur Kennedy. He is a frequent speaker at psychology, Jungian psychotherapy, and psychiatry conferences.

Thomas Wilmer is a freelance writer, travel correspondent, storyteller, and builder in San Luis Obispo, California. He is a frequent contributor to regional publications and is the travel editor of the *Five-Cities Times Press Recorder* in Arroyo Grande, California. He is a board member and travel correspondent for the NPR affiliate, KCBX Public Radio, serving San Luis Obispo and Santa Barbara counties. He is also on the Salvation Army's advisory board because of his concern for and efforts on behalf of the homeless.

Eleanora M. Woloy, M.D., is a psychiatrist and Jungian analyst practicing in Virginia Beach, Virginia. She is Associate Professor of Psychiatry at Eastern Virginia Medical School and lectures widely throughout the United States. Her medical degree was received from the University of Michigan School of Medicine in 1957. Dr. Woloy completed graduate training in adult psychiatry at Northville State Hospital in Detroit and in child psychiatry at Hawthorn Center in Livonia, Michigan. She earned her diploma in Jungian analysis through the Inter-Regional Society of Jungian Analysts. Her book, *The Symbol of the Dog in the Human Psyche*, was published in 1990.

CLOSENESS

in Personal and Professional Relationships

Introduction

This book contains chapters that were edited from lectures presented at the 1989 annual meeting of the Inter-Regional Society of Jungian Analysts, hosted by the Institute for the Humanities at Salado, Texas. The conference, which was dedicated to Joseph L. Henderson, the dean of American Jungian analysts, grew out of my offer to organize a meeting on the subject of closeness. For the book, I invited other authors to contribute chapters that I believed were necessary to round out the subject.[1]

Since the conference was in Texas, I had originally thought of calling it "Cactuses, Porcupines, and Other Prickly Things." Then I realized that people might think it was a convention for naturalists, so I opted for "Closeness." Yet the porcupines brought to mind these words of Arthur Schopenhauer:

> One cold winter's day, a number of porcupines huddled together quite closely in order through their mutual warmth to prevent themselves from being frozen. But they soon felt the effect of their quills on one another, which made them again move apart. Now when the need for warmth once more brought them together, the drawback of the quills was repeated so that they were tossed between two evils, until they had discovered the proper distance from which they could best tolerate one another. Thus the need for society which springs from the emptiness and monotony of men's lives, drives them together; but their many unpleasant and repulsive qualities and insufferable drawbacks once more drive them apart. The mean distance which they finally discover,

and which enables them to endure being together, is politeness and good manners.[2]

Closeness, then, is about intimacy and distance, decency and ethics. It is about attachment and loss, domination and dependency, transference and countertransference, touching and sex. Closeness is at the very heart of human relationships.

This theme seems to me to be one of the central issues of our times, in personal life to be sure, but especially in professional relations. Just how "close" can or should be the relationship between therapist and client, doctor and patient, teacher and student, supervisor and candidate? The message of this book focuses on relationships characterized by power imbalance and hierarchical order. It speaks not only to people in the fields of psychology and analysis, but to all individuals in the helping professions; to anyone interested in organizational psychology; to people in business, education, the ministry, and the military; to lovers and families.

Part One, "Therapist and Client," begins with June Singer's fascinating review of the subject of androgyny, contrasting Freudian and Jungian points of view. The anima and animus archetypes and the Jungian concept of the contrasexual unconscious are explained and illustrated by case material showing the tensions and understanding of both the analyst and the analysand and the healing power of the rituals of control.

Thomas Kirsch's sensitive and candid chapter, "The Analytic Relationship," relates discoveries he has made about the nature of the relationships of his patients to others and to himself. Differentiating between closeness within the analytic relationship and the phenomenon of transference, Kirsch addresses the issue of the analyst's self-disclosure to the patient. He describes his own personality and typology and shows how these affect his experiences of intimacy, connectedness, and love with his patients and how this is viewed within the real parameters of analysis.

The commentary by Kendra Crossen on "Closeness and the Patient" brings to the book the feeling reaction of a patient who sought the help of a Jungian analyst without the complication of being a candidate. She offers a literary, reflective observation of the anticipation and fantasy of the woman and man in analysis and reality. By drawing attention to the presence of love and silence, she reveals both space and relationship in the closeness of healing.

I have contributed a chapter on relationship and dreams of a psychologist patient who developed AIDS while in training analysis with me. I continued his treatment until his death, recording all of his dreams, the feeling tone of the analytic relationship, and its change as dictated by the reality of his physical illness and certain death. His role in the in-depth teaching video tape on AIDS made with professional caregivers was to him his legacy. Closeness was healing even to death.

The compelling poem by Carol Mouché is an expression of the pathos of a hidden inner dialogue when she was a psychotherapy patient. The inner dialogue of the patient may be inferred by the therapist, but it is far better to see the patient's own recollection of inner dialogue. It is equally useful for the therapist to become conscious of his or her own inner dialogue.

Peter Rutter, the author of *Sex in the Forbidden Zone*, writes on relationships of closeness and trust using the mythology of Hermes, Mercurius, Loki, and Coyote—the trickster, guardian of the boundary, and boundary-maker—to give a practical and theoretical Jungian perspective. The differentiation between sexual fantasy and overt sexual behavior distinguishes the boundaries of relationship in analysis. The real dangers of breaking through such boundaries by insensitive, hurtful actions, gestures, or comments are told in a straightforward manner by an analyst who knows the healing power in relationship.

"Confidentiality and Betrayal in the Therapy of Anne Sexton: A Dialogue with Diane Wood Middlebrook" presents a vivid and thoughtful discussion of the relationship of Sexton with two of her psychiatrists. The 1991 publication of Professor Middlebrook's biography of the well-known poet provoked a debate over the release of audio tapes of Sexton's therapy sessions to her biographer by one of the therapists, as well as the revelation of Sexton's affair with the other therapist. My essay is uncomplimentary to the first therapist and condemns the grossly unethical behavior of the second. The intriguing part of this chapter is the way "things" are hidden and how they are revealed. Incidentally, my dialogue with Professor Middlebrook in this chapter was drawn from an informal seminar at the Salado Institute that took place before the controversial biography was available to me; hence it is a candid discussion, unaffected by the furor in the press that occurred later.

Psychoanalyst Montague Ullman's chapter, "Image and Metaphor: Dreams in a Small-Group Setting," discusses the role of closeness in dream seminars he conducts in which all participants are on an equal level whether they are sharing their own dreams or helping to interpret someone else's. Ullman's ideas are original, creative, courageous, and free of doctrinal analytic jargon. They are intended to bring dream appreciation to the general public and for use in teaching dynamic psychotherapy. In creating a safe environment for the exploration of dreams,

Ullman shows us how the analysis of the unconscious can be examined following the disciplined rules of technique and conduct that define his groups, allowing emotional healing to take place in an interpersonal field.

"Transference/Countertransference" grew out of my seminars with psychiatric residents and psychology trainees at the University of Texas in a required course in analytical psychology. It is a manner of writing and speaking at the same time in free verse to people interested in learning the nuts and bolts of Jungian psychotherapy.

In Part Two, "Family and Society," Joseph L. Henderson's chapter on social attitude addresses the rituals of intitiation and cultural attitudes as archetypal phenomena. Through personal reflections and literary and clinical examples, Henderson shows us how the social attitude has three aspects—personal, cultural, and archetypal—and that the true individual is the true social person.

Eleanora M. Woloy draws our attention to the stereotypical roles and myths of man and woman, and particularly to the archetypal feminine principle. From informal interviews and clinical experience, Woloy concludes that the capacity for closeness in relationship proceeds from the central organizing archetype of the psyche, the Self.

Thomas Wilmer, my son, writes a chapter on being the "Son of a Psychiatrist." With sensitivity, affection, sincerity, and courage, he reveals how his analyst father's career and professional demands affected the family, especially my relationship with him. Tom tells of the satisfaction and relief he experienced when I changed from being a Freudian analyst to a Jungian analyst. This is a reflection not only of social attitudes and biases, but of the reality of the particularly orthodox classical Freudian world of San Francisco and how he saw its effect on me.

In "Closeness in Personal Relationship," Mary Ann

Mattoon writes on the varieties of modes and models of psychological relations, closeness, intimacy, sexual attraction, and love. She examines the nature of psychological relations, especially the notions of projections and individuation, within the conceptual frame of Jungian thought.

Starting off Part Three, "Among Professionals," Karl E. Weick's chapter on the organizational management of closeness in Jungian training societies brings his genius to bear on the conflicts that learned societies face when they must carry out the functions of both training and of judgment on a person's acceptance or rejection into the society. He comes close to suggesting that this is an impossible task, especially given the nature of the Inter-Regional Society, the largest Jungian society in the United States, with its expanse from coast to coast and from Canada to Nassau. The problematic issues of survival, subordination, and the inherent liaisons are so clearly presented that this chapter should be required reading for all who are concerned with training and learned societies.

In "The Candidate," James Shultz writes tactfully and wisely about role diffusion and trust, fairness and indiscretion. He describes the Inter-Regional Society's practice of conducting candidate interviews in an analyst's hotel room during annual meetings, with five or six analysts asking the one candidate penetrating questions. One cannot help wondering about such group interviews with their clear potential for the misuse of power. Shultz describes his own feeling of being "opened from stem to sternum." I have sat in on such group interviews and can attest to the distressing lack of sensitivity to group dynamics and the blindness to the shadow of power of some analysts.

Unfortunately, the deficiencies of such an analyst will mark the deficiency of the analysis, so that the candidate, like an abused child, when certified and sent out into the world is driven by the compulsion to find similar ways to abuse others in the name of analysis. That this is true of only a small number of analysts does not mitigate its importance. It is the conscious understanding of such phenomena and their correction that motivates this book—it is not an exposé but an attempt at an honest look both within and beyond the confines of an analytic society.

The companion chapter by Joseph Wakefield draws our attention to the power differentials and explains his own painful learning experiences as a supervisor. He draws our attention to his view of the tensions in supervision in regard to openness, self-disclosure, and the complications of playing the dual role of supervisor and judge with the power to fail the candidate. He elaborates on these ideas from the perspective of a variety of psychological schools of thought. In the supervisor's overview of Jungian societies by surveys, it is important to note that these are impressionistic inquiries of rumors, not facts. Although the information is therefore hearsay, it nonetheless should alert the reader to the abuse of power by analysts, including sexual exploitation and seduction of any sort.

The final poem is my reflection on the emotional impact of coming to the end of analysis from the point of view of the analysand. This is often spoken of as "termination," but it is not "terminal" but rather separation and a new beginning.

It is hoped that this book will contribute to the necessary openness in examining ethical issues related to closeness, intimacy, and distance as seen from a variety of experiences. But always there is our conscience and shadow as our necessary, even if unwelcome, teachers. Jung wrote:

Conscience, and particularly bad conscience, can be a gift from heaven, a veritable grace if used in the interests of the higher self-criticism. And self-criticism, in the sense of an introspective, discriminating activity, is indispensable in any attempt to understand your own psychology. If you have done something that puzzles you and you ask yourself what could have prompted you to such an action, you need the sting of a bad conscience and its discriminating faculty in order to discover the real motives of your behaviour. It is only then that you can see what motives are governing your actions. The sting of a bad conscience even spurs you on to discover things that were unconscious before, and in this way you may be able to cross the threshold of the unconscious and take cognizance of those imper-sonal forces which make you an unconscious instrument of the wholesale murderer in man.[3]

Harry A. Wilmer

NOTES

1. I would like to thank Elizabeth Juden and Paige Britt for their editorial assistance in preparing the book for publication.
2. Arthur Schopenhauer, *Parerga and Paralipomena: Short Philo-sophical Essays*, vol. 1, trans. E. F. J. Payne (Oxford: Claren-don Press, 1974). Cited in Harry A. Wilmer, *A Dictionary of Ideas: Closeness* (Salado, Tex.: Institute for the Humanities with Merrill Webster Publishing, 1989), p. ix.
3. C. G. Jung, *Psychology and Religion*, CW 11, p. 49, para. 86.

Part One

THERAPIST
AND PATIENT

Closeness and Androgyny

June Singer

> When you make the two one, and when you make the
> inside like the outside and the outside like the inside, and
> the above like the below, and when you make the male and
> the female one and the same, so that the male not be male
> nor the female . . . then will you enter the kingdom.
>
> —*The Gospel of Thomas*[1]

Androgyny is an ideal state.
Being male or being female is a material reality for
human beings.

These two propositions sound simple enough, but in
the process of living, they become hopelessly intertwined.
If we could think of ourselves as *creatures* like the rest of
the vertebrates, with sexual organs that clearly identified
us as belonging to one sex and only to that sex, it would
be simple indeed. But human beings are unique among
animals in that we generate ideas that, in turn, generate
ideals. Once we begin to conceptualize something, we
begin to think about what it could be or what it should
be. Recognizing our own sexual gifts, we soon begin to
notice what we do not have (e.g., we acquire "penis envy"
or "womb envy" in its real or symbolic manifestations).
While the Freudian camp suggests that this longing results
in neuroses, Jungians tend to believe that it signifies a

yearning toward wholeness. Perhaps my own analytical training has prejudiced me in favor of the latter view, but this has been reinforced by my investigations into the history and mythologies of many societies in which androgyny, the *psychological* integration of masculinity and femininity, was conceptualized as an ideal state.

Human propensities to think, contemplate, and evaluate set us apart from those animals who are blessed in their naiveté when it comes to matters of sexuality and gender identification. While other animals seem reasonably content just doing what comes naturally, the human animal seems destined to elaborate to infinity the physical and psychological functions related to sex roles and sexual behavior—until the shelves of our bookstores overflow with poetry, fiction, and essays on the subject, museums and galleries cover their walls with sexual metaphors, and stage, screen, and musical performances all the way from grand opera to rap glorify or damn all forms of intercourse between the sexes. For psychotherapists, sex and relationships are the bread and butter of the profession. Since human beings are thinking beings, the bare facts of material reality fail to satisfy us. There exists in us an unquenchable thirst for ideas that will propel us toward something better than what we have and that which we conceive of as "ideal." One such ideal is androgyny.

Androgyny is a common term today, and much has been written about it. When my book *Androgyny*[2] was first published in 1976, few people were familiar with the term. Those who were tended to confuse it with bisexuality (the tendency to choose members of both sexes as sexual partners) or hermaphroditism (a physiological abnormality in which both male and female reproductive organs are present in an individual). Later on, when "unisex" came into vogue, androgyny was understood as a sort of ambiguity, either in appearance or manner, that made men appear "womanish" or women appear "mannish." None of these ideas about androgyny remotely resembles what I have in mind when I use the word. Androgyny, as I understand it and as I will employ it here, refers to an ideal of *psychological* wholeness in which both males and females regard themselves first as human beings and only secondarily as men or as women.

To come to this position requires that individuals stop limiting themselves to roles or tasks or ideas that are "sex-appropriate" and that they refrain from placing limits upon other people based upon sexually stereotypical ideas or behaviors. This cannot be done until we are able to come to terms with what has long been called the "*unconscious* contrasexual opposite" and begin to integrate this into a *consciousness* that is evolving toward androgyny. I hasten to say that my concept of androgyny does not devalue the generative and nurturance functions, but neither does it isolate these as the sole responsibility of one sex. Outside of the physical necessities of pregnancy, giving birth, and breast-feeding, I believe that most of the activities associated with parenting can and should be the shared concern and responsibility of men and women. Today this may seem obvious, and in many families it is taken for granted; but in the workplace, it is certainly not a foregone conclusion that all employers will provide for male and female workers alike whatever may be necessary to make it possible for them to be productive at work without sacrificing parenting. The guiding principle of androgyny is that all human beings should have the right, if they so desire, to exercise those natural aspects of their natures which, for the sake of expediency, have been assigned by our society to one sex or the other. We cannot bring the inner opposites together unless we also bring the outer opposites together, for we are all of a piece and we suffer greatly when we try to force a division in ourselves.

If we accept androgyny as an ideal, it is clear that social changes must follow, and we may not be ready for them. We are still reeling from the fallout of the sexual liberation of the sixties, the women's liberation movement of the seventies, and the regression to archaic power-fantasies in the eighties that led many people to identify with the gods and goddesses, witches and magicians, wild women and wild men that captivated their imaginations. In this last decade of the millennium, we are trying to regain a balance in the midst of radical changes in values and in the nature of human relationships.

Individuals who in the past have thought of themselves as disenfranchised for one reason or another are now seeking to claim their own power, exhibiting a tendency to idealize aspects of their own gender and to identify with these idealized images. In the process of identifying with their own sex, they frequently reject the values and behavioral modes of the opposite sex and consequently, they begin to isolate themselves emotionally, intellectually, or spiritually from their contrasexual opposites—both within and without. Their former closeness with their partners may be put aside in favor of a stance that appears to them to be more valuable to society at large, or more archetypal, or more congruent to their true natures. For better or for worse, this ideological shift does not greatly affect the more basic aspects of physical closeness with members of the opposite sex. Physically, we enjoy closeness and seek it out; ideologically we long to be whole and believe that to evolve in this direction, we must become self-sufficient and independent. Herein may lie one source of the tension between the material reality and the idea or the ideal.

This tension of the opposites is felt most intensely today

by psychologically sophisticated people who are reasonably mature on an ego level, and who are fully sexual beings with a degree of self-understanding, a sense of interiority, and feeling of self-fulfillment in the external world. In midlife or beyond, they have completed the first half of the individuation process, have found an identity for themselves that they can live with, and have learned to make their way in the world. They take maleness or femaleness for granted and, if they give any further thought to it, that thought goes toward enhancing their images of themselves as masculine or feminine.

In my analytic practice, I am often struck by an ambivalence in both male and female clients who have already experienced themselves in the sex roles that society has assigned to them and have found a way to liberate themselves from the stereotypes that these roles entail. But instead of embracing their contrasexual aspects and therefore their androgyny, they appear to be trying hard to deepen their one-sided sexual identity. It is as though they wanted to exchange the feminine stereotype for the feminine archetype, or the masculine stereotype for the masculine archetype.

How might this work out in everyday life? Women born after the Second World War no longer identify themselves with the fifties image of the housewife that their mothers modeled for them. They have been persuaded that this image is one of powerlessness, to the point that they no longer believe that "the hand that rocks the cradle rules the world." (I don't believe it unequivocally, either, but I do see the importance of shaping the world of the future through faithfully and intelligently guiding our children—a task, as I have suggested, that can be performed equally well by both men and women.) Women who believe that they have been socialized to be powerless now want to identify with feminine images of power: witches and priestesses and goddesses by the dozen. For those not so mythically minded, there is Wonderwoman, who *does* it all, or Princess Diana, who *has* it all. These women are, of course, supported by the current spate of books, lectures, and workshops on "woman power."

Men have also begun to identify more consciously with male archetypes, perhaps in reaction to this trend. From goddesses to gods, the images in our society shift according to the sex of the one who is doing the imagining. Men are fascinated to read about the most outrageous uses and abuses of power these days. Now that liberated women have reinvented the matriarchy, newly liberated men are reinventing the patriarchy.

When this shoring up of our gender identification goes to extremes, some individuals take on a quality of male or female identification that depreciates the values commonly associated with the opposite sex. These individuals then can find themselves caught in a strange paradox: the "independent" aspect of the psyche longs for freedom from responsibility to another person in an intimate relationship, eschews commitments, and wants very much to have time and space for being alone; while, at the same time, these women or men are aware, almost to obsession, of a need for closeness to another person. This need for closeness may conceal a neurotic dependence for which the conscious longing for "freedom" is compensatory. However, in a healthy, balanced person who respects and sustains both the inner and the outer contrasexual element, this longing for freedom is a desire for at-one-ness. This at-one-ness means being at one with the rest of the universe, with the systems within systems that are ordered by a cosmic harmony so vast that it outstrips the capacity of the human mind to deal with it. Immense and full of wonder as this wholeness is, and inaccessible as it seems to most of us, like the sun it provides life-giving power for everything that lives. That this transpersonal awareness *can* be accomplished within the context of a warm and loving relationship is convincing evidence of our androgynous nature, which endows every human being with the potential for being while in oneself and also with the ability to experience closeness in relationship with another. Bringing these opposites together, as I see it, is one of the major tasks and goals of the second half of the individuation process.

In my recent book, *Seeing through the Visible World*,[3] I proposed that we exist in two worlds simultaneously. ("This" or "this world" will be used here to denote the visible world of consciousness, while "that" or "that world" will refer to what I have called "the invisible world," or "the unknowable.") The first is the visible world of material, where we deal with the practical events of everyday life. This is the "known world." It contains everything we know, that is, it is the realm of consciousness. In addition, this first world contains the "knowable," which includes everything that people are likely to discover through the efforts of the intellect and through personal experience.

The second world, the invisible world, is of a different logical order altogether. It cannot be approached by the intellect alone, for it is "unknowable" through intellect. That second world is the invisible matrix from which this visible world emerges. There, where there is neither time nor space and where nothing is visible to the eyes of the senses, are the ordering principles, the desire for life and the ultimate source of energy. If there is a God out there, it is an alien, an indescribable and unknowable God, a universal God who might be thought of as the archetype after which all the local gods of humankind are fashioned. Jung understood that world as the archetypal world, which is truly unconscious, so that all that we can say about it is derived from its manifestations in this world and from our reflections upon them. Yet we, with our insatiable desire to search for what is beyond our grasp, know in a deep, intuitive way that there is that other world, even though we cannot reach out and touch it. Like Michelangelo's Adam on the ceiling of the Sistine Chapel, our hands reach out toward the fingers of God, but we cannot quite make contact with them, and yet there is an invisible spark that flows between that Mysterious Other and ourselves. It is that tension between propinquity and separation that gives us life. In the very act of giving life to humankind, the tension of the opposites is also transferred to us.

I believe that we human beings have always known that we exist in the two worlds simultaneously: this world, and that world. This world is all around us, and we experience it through all our senses and through the devices we employ to extend our senses beyond the range of our physical limitations. These devices include microscopes and telescopes, computers and space probes, radio and television, and so on. All of these "prosthetic devices" serve to enlarge our *sense* perceptions of the visible world. The invisible world cannot be reached by any of these methods, for no matter how much we know or are able to learn, the unknowable always recedes beyond the boundaries of the known and the knowable. Children are closer to that world than are most adults. Children are able to engage the most outrageous fantasies and live in them. But in the process of socializing our children, we carefully teach them what is "real" and what is fantasy or impossible or is a lie, and they soon learn to repress that wondrous capacity to see what adults do not see. It takes adults a very long time and a committed cultivation of the function of intuition to be able to regain that capacity to see beyond the visible world. Nevertheless, by the time they have reached midlife, most adults experience the feeling that they have missed out on something very important. Sometimes that something appears to be outside of them, but on closer inspection, the source of the longing is discovered to be within. It has to do with the mysterious contrasexual archetype that Jung called the *anima* when it is experienced in men, and the *animus* in women. But of course it appears in many guises, and just calling it anima or animus is simply labeling something that is far too subtle and too pervasive to be dismissed so easily. An exploration into the invisible world of the unconscious is called for, and this cannot take place through the usual methods of scientific exploration because the unconscious does not submit to controlled experimentation. What Jung called "analysis" is not analytical in the sense of taking something apart and examining it piece by piece, but rather a process something like that of a cat who sits by a mouse hole patiently, expectantly, and alertly, waiting for the quarry to emerge.

If an important aspect of Jungian analysis, or "analytical psychology," is the process of coming to terms with the anima or animus, then it follows that this must constitute one of the major themes of the analytic encounter. Whether the analyst is of the same sex or the opposite sex from the analysand affects the manner in which this tension will be lived out in the analytic hour, but it must be lived out in either case. In same-sex analytic relationships, the analysand's primary encounter may be with the contrasexual aspect of the analyst, while in opposite-sex analytic relationships, the first encounter is more likely to be with the ego of the analyst. In either situation, the stage is set for acting out the tension between the desire to closeness with the contrasexual other and the desire to integrate the contrasexual in oneself. *What has been insufficiently recognized in the past, I believe, is that this tension is just as profound and pervading in the analyst as it is in the analysand.*

This tension surely is a major source of transference and countertransference in analysis. Harry Wilmer, in his eminently clear and practical discussion of transference and countertransference, says:

> What lies deeply buried in the psyche beyond conscious comprehension is experienced outside in someone else. . . . Every therapist encounters transference. Every therapist experiences countertransference, irrational thoughts and feelings about the patient, but not all face transference and countertransference. Many about-face to save face.[4]

Issues arising from unconscious handling of transference and countertransference have become the active concern of analytic training institutes throughout the United States recently. There have been incidents in which unconscious feelings, especially in but not limited to the sexual area, have been acted out in some psychotherapy relationships, and the cry has been raised for better training of therapists and analysts concerning the unconscious relationships that evolve in the course of therapy or analysis. Codes of ethics have been written or are being written or revised, and seminars have been instituted to deal with the many ethical questions that arise in the closeness of the analytic connection. Much has been written about the erotic transference/countertransference, but not enough about the more subtle ways in which the unconscious contrasexual other arises in the course of analytic work. I will cite a case in which these more subtle issues arose, but first I want to sharpen the difference between analytic training today and that of a generation ago.

In the course of my analytic training at the Jung Institute of Zurich early in the 1960s, I learned very little about transference and countertransference, except for what was extrapolated from Jung's commentary on the illustrations in a sixteenth-century alchemical text, the *Rosarium Philosophorum*.[5] That esoteric document used alchemical imagery to symbolize the mysterious basis of the *opus*, which Jung equated with the psychological work of the individuation process. Several stages are described, during which the elements emerge within the "primordial chaos," which is also called "the vessel" or "the uterus."[6] The "masculine" is portrayed there as the "active resolve or *agens* whose alchemical equivalent is the 'upwelling,' " and the "feminine" is characterized as the "receptive, absorbent *patiens*, or the material that still has to be formed and impregnated."[7] These and other elements pass through a series of transformations in which they become differentiated from each other and then, eventually, are able to combine in the "conjunction of opposites" that represents the goal of the alchemical and, presumably, the psychological process. The long process leading from the original and primitive order of human society to an inner order of the psyche is delineated in alchemical terms that point toward the goal of the androgynous Self which is total and timeless, and which stands for the mutual integration of consciousness and the unconscious.[8]

In my own analysis, we proceeded through various stages. These were ritualized events, and although I did not view them as contemporary expressions of the *Rosarium*, they nevertheless held great importance for me. For example, my analyst used to take her analysands out to dinner once a year. It was a sort of courtly rite of passage marking the anniversary of the analysis. Today, if anyone from an ethics committee were to see analyst and analysand dining together in a restaurant, they would probably speak privately to the analyst in question, raise the sleeping monster of "dual relationship," and suggest that such a practice be immediately discontinued. I must admit that I did entertain certain fantasies of a more private tête-à-tête following some of those dinners, but of course they never happened, and I do not believe that I was any worse for having thought such unthinkable thoughts.

Another experience relating to transference/countertransference issues came on the first day that I saw a certain male analyst to discuss the possibility of my working analytically with him. In Zurich we were required to work with analysts of both sexes. I had chosen this particular analyst because I had heard him lecture and noted that he bore a strong resemblance to my grandfather, whom I adored. I fell madly in love with the analyst as a consequence, but of course I gave no clue to this when I went for my initial interview. The analyst may have been more intuitive than I had imagined, for in that hour he said gently to me, "I want you to know beforehand that my wife is a psychologist and I often discuss my cases with her." This, of course, put me on notice that there would be no "funny business" in our work together. His remark was all to the good and set me at ease, but what I did not recognize then, and do now, is that what he was doing (discussing a case without express written permission) would today be considered a breach of confidentiality, not to mention a dilution of the transference.

My first control case (conducted under the supervision of a senior analyst) had left her former analyst because of certain sexually suggestive behaviors on his part. But neither of us imagined that this was anything about which to make a formal complaint (especially if you were still in training), and besides, there was no such thing as an "ethics committee" to whom you could safely complain. It was generally understood that if you didn't like the way an analyst behaved, you should take it upon yourself to leave that analyst and find another. I also remember one Jungian conference at which a distinguished analyst talked about how important it is for every analyst to have someone with whom it would be possible to talk in perfect freedom. "You have to find an analyst you can trust completely," he said. Then he paused and added, "But where can you find such an analyst?" The remark of course brought down the house. These few examples will serve to illustrate the level of consciousness about transference/countertransference issues in the sixties, when many of the Jungian analysts were trained who are now training the analysts of the future.

Today, I am happy to note, there is much more earnest talk and reflection about boundary issues in analysis and about transference and countertransference. Concerns about these areas are receiving a great deal of attention today in the training of Jungian analysts. Furthermore, conferences such as the one on "Closeness" are an important step in the process of coming to an awareness of the issues around relationships in the analytic frame. These conferences provide a setting in which analysts in practice can together examine their own work as they were sitting with their clients, and reflect on the elusive and implied messages they have been giving to their clients with every word, look, and gesture. It was not always thus, and it has taken the bitter experience of failed analyses and wounded souls to bring to the fore the sensitivity of these issues and the necessity to confront them. I can still recall a moment in my own training when I asked my control analyst,

"How can an analyst really know whether what he or she is doing is 'ethical' or not?" He answered me simply, "If you would feel comfortable having all your colleagues know about it, then you can be sure it's ethical." I still think this is good advice—possibly more useful and certainly more succinct than any elaborate ethical code.

With all the personal analytic work, and the training and seasoning in the therapist's chair, occasions occur when an analyst is overtaken by the power of the unconscious process and transgresses boundaries of the analytic relationship. Such "acting-out" behavior is no longer acceptable to the current generation of analysts and analysands, if indeed it ever was. That Jung himself carried on a strong personal relationship with a former analysand long after the analysis had terminated can be understood against the background that Jung was a pioneer exploring unmapped regions of the unconscious where no one had trodden before. Now, nearly a century after he saw his first patient, we have a far clearer idea of the pits and traps that exist there, and we have devised rituals to protect ourselves and our analysands. These include the following.

1. The boundary of time. The analytic hour is limited to a certain number of minutes, and both analyst and analysand learn to adhere to the discipline of containing the work in this limited span.

2. The boundary of space. The analytic hour takes place in the consulting room and only there, in a room set aside specifically for the purpose of the analytic encounter.

3. The ritual of the hour. The meeting occurs at the appointed time and in a manner that clearly establishes the purpose of the encounter as distinct from encounters with friends or lovers, or parent-child or teacher-student encounters.

4. The principle of nonduality of relationships. The analytic relationship is the only relationship that exists between analyst and analysand. There are no other tangential relationship, no business, no barter, no social relationships, nothing that is not directly related to the analysis.

5. The final boundary is the recognition that although an analytic relationship may be formally terminated, the emotional alliance may endure indefinitely. It is quite possible that some former analysands may become friends of their analysts, but for others, this may block off the possibility that analytic work might be resumed in the future. The problem is that at the time of termination, one can never be sure into which category a given analytical relationship may fall. For that reason, extreme care needs to be taken in developing other kinds of relationships with former analysands or analysts.

Despite the naiveté in this area with which I began my analytic practice in the mid-sixties, my experiences over the past twenty-five years in the work have taught me a great deal about transference-countertransference. I recently received a letter from a former analysand, "Anton" (not his real name), with whom I worked near the beginning of my years of analytic practice. In the time since the analysis was terminated, he had written to me from time to time to let me know how he was getting along in his professional life and with his wife and children. Over the years, he continued to pay attention to his dreams, noting them down carefully and seriously reflecting upon them; he kept up with Jungian literature and identified his thinking as "Jungian," although he had added to it much from the spiritual discipline that is central in his work. From his letters over the years, I gained the impression that he and

his wife experienced "closeness" in the area of their domestic life and that they were compatible sexually and in
the practical matters of everyday living. Now, at midlife,
"Anna" was beginning to grow restive in her waning
domestic role and was visited by some disturbing dreams.
In his letter Anton wrote out one of Anna's recent dreams.
The dream content is not important here, but the question
he raised is. What would I think of his working with his
wife on her dreams? "After all," he said, "I have had so
many years of experience working on my own dreams,
and while I'm not an analyst, I feel fairly comfortable
about the way I understand dreams."

Anton fit perfectly the above situation (5), in which the
analysis had ended many years ago, or so I thought. The
occasional letters that passed between us could easily be
understood as just a friendly way of keeping in touch, a
periodic progress report. But now it becomes clear that
these letters also served as a method of keeping a channel
open through which we might once more communicate
on matters of depth should the occasion for this arise. I
myself had doubted the statement I had read a short time
ago in a proposed draft of an ethics code for analysts, that
some analytic relationships last *forever*, but now I was not
so willing to nay say it.

I might have asked, in the past, "Why is it necessary to
have all these rules and controls?" Now I think I would
have an answer for this question. We have learned through
our own experience as analysts and as analysands that true
freedom cannot exist except where there is discipline.
When children are told that they can do anything they
want, they are often frightened at the thought that there
are no boundaries, that no one will tell them how far they
can safely go. Consequently, they may either run wild,
testing the limits, or sit timidly in a corner, fearing to

venture into the unknown. But when they are given a protected playground and a fixed amount of time to spend there, they can feel safe enough to exercise their freedoms. Digging in the depths of the soul can be a dangerous business, and analysts have learned (or should have learned) to provide the necessary safeguards to protect the relationship between themselves and their analysands.

It is an interesting phenomenon, and one exemplified in the case of Anton, that analysands may leave the active analytic process after what is thought by them and by the analyst to be a "successful termination," and then they go out into the world believing that they know quite a bit about the analytic process. From their own perspective, they do, but from the perspective of the analyst, they may not. They are quite innocent of the inner work that their analyst has been doing on himself or herself through every hour and every minute of the time spent sitting with the analysand. They do not realize that it is only because the analyst is personally disinterested or noninvolved in the everyday life of the analysand that the analysis works. It is not that the analyst doesn't care what happens, but rather that the analyst does not have a vested interest in the analytic process turning out a certain way. Analysts learn to allow the unconscious to inform consciousness as to the direction the process should take in order for the wholeness of the individual to manifest. Then the transpersonal Self can work with the personal ego to bring about a harmonious experience of the whole. But for the analysand, the whole exploration has been primarily one of self-interest. The analysand is seeking *wholeness*, which is the meaning of individuation, no matter what it costs. Many sacrifices are made in the cultivation of these fruits. It is like the "experience" of which William Blake was thinking when he wrote:

What is the price of Experience? Do men buy it for a song?
Or wisdom for a dance in the street?
No, it is bought with the price of all that a man hath, his
wife, his children.
Wisdom is sold in the desolate market where none come
to buy,
And in the wither'd field where the farmer plows for
bread, in vain.[9]

Like any person who has gone through the long and difficult work of analysis, making radical changes in life-style in the process, Anton had a huge investment in his own individuation. Through the force of his personality, he is able to influence others, and he is held in respect by his congregants and his colleagues. Many people come to him for advice and counsel, not only because he is their minister but also because of his understanding of psychological issues and his clarity in discussing them. He knows that he has to be careful, however, to keep his relationships with his congregants as conscious as possible. When he meets with individuals in the privacy of his study to discuss their personal problems with them, he is aware that these are the same people he will see at parties, on the church board, or in community affairs, and so he must be cautious about the possibility of developing a strong unconscious relationship with these people. Of course in such a relationship, it is nearly impossible *not* to develop a strong unconscious relationship, but there are ways to bring this to consciousness both in himself and in those with whom he counsels, and the earlier in the relationship the better.

Clergy belong to a group of people who are especially prone to receive projections of the spiritual or intellectual animus of women, and of the gentle and tender anima of men. Also found in this group are analysts, physicians, teachers, and others whose role tends to be that of mentor or counselor. The kind of closeness that develops here is a function of the natural thrust toward androgyny, in which the woman seeks in the object of her affection the realization of her own undeveloped spiritual or intellectual animus, while the man seeks in his projection object the realization of his feminine side or anima, which represents his undeveloped tenderness or empathy.

Anton was sensitive to this possibility, and whenever he noticed that this kind of projection was taking place he would make conscious the necessity for holding the tension between closeness and androgyny, in order that the person might recognize the projection as evidence of the need to develop within himself or herself the very aspects that he or she would be attracted to so profoundly in Anton. Furthermore, Anton wisely had not attempted to work with the dreams of his congregants, possibly because of an instinctive feeling that he might get into deeper water than he could safely swim in.

His relationship with Anna, however, was another matter. Ostensibly, in suggesting that he work with her on her dreams, he would do so in the spirit of "helping" her. But would this really be helpful? Could a man be disinterested and objective with someone with whom he was sleeping every night, who bore his children and kept his home in order and whom he needed to fulfill many of the "feminine" functions in his life? Could he be disinterested and objective with a woman for whom he cared deeply and whom he did not want to hurt or discipline or control—at least not consciously? What about all the boundaries that might be transgressed?

I cannot speak about Anna's role here since I do not know her, but I can speculate, on the basis of my experience with other wives of articulate and charismatic men, wives who have not yet found their own voice. I imagined that such a woman might look upon her husband as wiser, more articulate, and more experienced in handling human relationships than she felt herself to be. She might rely on him to make most of the decisions in their mutual lives because of a fear that she could not measure up to his exacting standards and a wish to avoid his criticism. Her fears could surface in disturbing dreams, sufficient to make her husband feel that she needed help in coming to some understanding of them.

Any married couple carries a variety of conscious and unconscious feelings toward one another that they may not always wish to disclose or share, especially the negative ones. Each knows that the other must have negative feelings that he or she may not express. This is particularly true for a woman who is economically dependent on her husband. There could be many feelings rising up in her with respect to her husband that she feels she had better bury in a corner somewhere. When she makes the midlife transition from active mothering to facing the necessity of discovering or deciding just who she might be as an individual, the dreaming unconscious could be strongly activated. I speculated that a woman in this position might now be nurturing a neo-nascent sense of self. She would need protection for the unrealized side of her that, if it could be developed, would complete the androgynous whole.

As a person who liked to be "in charge" of most of his relationships and one to whom people looked for guidance, Anton thought he ought to be able to analyze Anna's dreams. Could he have been aware, I asked myself, or was it just below his threshold of consciousness, that were he to probe the deep waters of Anna's dreaming unconscious, he might find some dragons there that he would not like to see? Might he not be threatened by this incipient development? It is likely that he would be far too "mature" to own such insecurity in himself, so it must remain unconscious. He might displace his ambivalance around the possibility of his wife's becoming a fully developed individual with needs and wants and aspirations of her own, onto his desire to help her. But in reality, could not the "help" also be a means of monitoring and controlling her development? Could not the very closeness that exists between them stand in the way of a fully androgynous development in Anna? Moreover, in Anton's efforts to cultivate the psyche of the woman in his life, might he not be avoiding the cultivation of his own anima qualities: her pliability, her interiority, and her willingness to nurture without the expectation of reward?

I imagined the temptation that would exist for Anton to "interpret" Anna's dreams in ways that would support his conscious and unconscious agenda for her and for himself. The possibility that he would claim, again overtly or unconsciously, to know her better than she knew herself, loomed large. Here was a perfect opportunity to exercise the power of a quicker intellect to "know better" under the guise of "helping."

I felt fully justified in replying to Anton's letter with a strong negative—I did not think it a good idea for him to try to analyze his wife's dreams. I thought that she would be far better off working with an analyst or, if that was not possible, for her to reflect on her dreams alone—perhaps with the help of a good book like Jungian analyst Karen Signell's *Wisdom of the Heart: Working with Women's Dreams*,[10] which presents many dreams and suggests a variety of possibilities in dealing with them. Then Anna might be able to take responsibility for exploring her own dreams, with many examples before her of how the process might work. She might find her own androgyny through her own active seeking.

In conclusion, I would like to return to our initial theme, "When you make the two one . . . and when you make the male and the female one and the same, so that the male will not be male nor the female female. . . ." As I understand it, this quotation from the Gospel of Thomas suggests that the ideal state, the state of perfection, is androgynous. We must move in the direction of uniting the masculine and the feminine aspects of our nature, so that the inner tension between these will no longer have to be projected onto the persons who are closest to us. But it must be remembered that androgyny is an ideal, a direction in which to move as we seek personal development. Meanwhile, between now and the time we enter the Kingdom of Heaven, we still live in a sexual world, and we still long for another to help us fill out aspects of ourselves that remain incompletely developed. It seems possible to me that we can enjoy the delights of closeness with another person while, at the same time, recognizing that person's impulse toward wholeness and respecting it, just as we treasure our own many-faceted sexual beings as images, not yet fully realized, of the androgynous diamond body.

NOTES

1. James M. Robinson, ed., *The Nag Hammadi Library* (San Francisco: Harper & Row, 1988), p. 129.

2. June Singer, *Androgyny*, 1st ed. (Garden City, N.Y.: Anchor Press/Doubleday, 1976). The second edition, titled *Androgyny: The Opposites Within* (Boston: Sigo Press, 1989), is completely revised with a new introduction.

3. June Singer, *Seeing through the Visible World* (San Francisco: Harper & Row, 1990).

4. Harry A. Wilmer, *Practical Jung* (Wilmette, Ill.: Chiron Publications, 1987), p. 28.

5. C. G. Jung, "An Account of the Transference Phenomena Based on the Illustrations to the *Rosarium Philosophorum*" (1946), in *The Practice of Psychotherapy, Collected Works* 16 (Princeton, N.J.: Princeton University Press, 1966), pp. 163–321.

6. Ibid., para. 402.

7. Ibid., para. 407.

8. Ibid., para. 539.

9. "The Four Zoas," in *The Complete Writings of William Blake*, ed. Geoffrey Keynes (New York: Random House, 1957), p. 290.

10. Karen Signell, *Wisdom of the Heart: Working with Women's Dreams* (New York: Bantam Books, 1990).

The Analytic Relationship

~⁄~

Thomas B. Kirsch

Closeness is one of the many words in our vocabulary that describes a feeling of intimacy, connectedness, relatedness, love, and "related" expressions. It is not a part of the usual psychological language, but when it was used as the title of a conference at the Institute for the Humanities at Salado in October 1989, it worked to make the group feel "closer" to one another, much more so by the end of the conference. Closeness—its presence or absence in our lives—is a major concern for all of us: as a therapist I deal with its multiple configurations every day.

Particularly, I *experience* the quality of closeness that a patient brings to me and lives with me in the analysis. At the outset, I wish to differentiate closeness within the analytical relationship from transference. As Jung pointed out in many places, the analytical relationship includes both the transference-countertransference relationship and a real relationship. Most attention has been paid to the more unconscious transference-countertransference relationship, and deservedly so, as it provides the fulcrum of the analysis of the unconscious. The more conscious relational factors are generally lumped together as an afterthought and indeed are less often discussed. My aim here will be to concentrate on these "real" parameters of analysis. Obviously, it will be impossible to completely isolate the conscious factors of a "real" relationship from the unconscious ones, as the transference is such a powerful force in all of depth psychotherapy and because the unconscious itself is a reality. In spite of this difficulty, I think there is some value in trying to tease out some of the conscious parameters in the analytical field.

As I began to let the issue of closeness come into focus in my practice, I began to think of all of my patients in terms of their own degree of closeness with others. I discovered to my surprise that a large majority of them (more than 60 percent) were not involved with a significant other. More than 60 percent of my patients were not only not married, they were not living with someone, nor were they in a serious relationship of any sort. Yet most of them would have liked to be in a serious, committed relationship, and many of them had joined dating services of various sorts in an effort to find a partner. It came as a shock to me to realize how many of my analysands did not have a significant other in their lives. I had always imagined that my practice was full of people with troubled relationships and that analysis was a way people chose, initially, to help them to understand and to cope with their difficult relationships. What I realized, with a start, was that the therapeutic relationship was for a majority of my patients the major and, many times, the *only* place where closeness and intimacy were experienced. I retained the hope that the therapeutic exchange could be more than an end in itself and would hopefully serve as some kind of model for future relationships in the world.

I asked several of my colleagues about their practices. Most of them did not have as high a percentage of single, uninvolved people. The colleagues I queried were mostly strong introverts, generally thinking intuitive types: I stood in contrast to them, with my strong extraverted intuitive feeling bias.

This difference in our practices led me to wonder about psychological type in relationship to the need for closeness in analysis. Perhaps my extraverted intuitive feeling attracted more isolated people who would feel protected by me, given the way I am apt to relate to people in therapy by reaching toward them. My combination of extraverted intuition and positive mother complex has tended to mean that I *have* to reach out to my patients to get to know them, which is not always in their best interests, I am aware. Obviously, the treatment situation involves my own countertransference as well as my psychological type. One young woman who relied upon my extraverted intuitive communication of feeling would feel an at absolute loss when I was quiet, neither engaging her in dialogue nor responding to her challenges. It has taken us many years to have some understanding about what it means when I do not respond, when I am simply feeling the patient in an introverted way without explanation from my extraverted intuition.

When this need for an ongoing feeling connection was expressed several times a week by many different patients, it became clear to me that my psychological type had much to do with the expectations patients have of me. I am reminded of what Joseph Wheelwright, the consummate extravert in his use of the feeling function, said so many times in his years of active practice: that he preferred to work "close in" with his patients. I understood him to mean then that he *had* to feel an emotional connection, otherwise the work was of no value to him. Now I realize that his patients must have been more comfortable, too. My own approach, overall, is much more introverted than Jo's, but I do sense what he meant by the feeling connection and how it becomes a reality when the therapist has extroverted feeling. I find I look for the emotional context even of dream material in the outer world as well as the inner world.

Over the years, my own extraversion has been balanced by my having had almost all of a very long analysis with an introverted intuitive thinking analyst. I well remember that in the beginning, he seemed so distant and remote to me. I felt validated by him, but the initial sense of distance took some time to overcome. Over time, however, I have become extremely close to him, and I treasure the various levels of our relationship. Our closeness, however, evolved slowly; early in analysis, I often wondered if I bored him with my emphasis on relationship issues. I now see that he was being less responsive to my extraversion. Gradually, my own responses in analytic work have become more naturally introverted, and I seem to listen differently to my patients. I am less pulled toward extraverted engagement, and I am more comfortable staying with the inner process in both of us. Often the silence leads to a breakthrough of the unconscious in a new way, and I can trust that now.

I have often wondered whether a certain psychological type enhanced closeness while others did not. Might feeling and intuition enhance closeness, while thinking and sensation produce distance in the analytic relationship? Does extraversion increase closeness and introversion allow for a certain distance in the analytic relationship? This train of thought led me to a thorny question in type theory: was one particular type better than another? Although type theory is supposedly without a value connotation, subtly certain psychological types have been more valued within the Jungian community. At one time, to be anybody in analytical psychology, it was almost necessary to be intuitive and introverted. If one had *neither* of these qualities well developed, one felt very much the outsider in Jungian circles. Extraversion and sensation were generally suspect, as people who were strong in these areas were often seen as less "deep." My own experience, both as an analysand and as an analyst, has led me to believe that no one psychological type has the inside track on closeness.

Another typical patient for me, practicing as I do in an area with a large concentration of business related to the microchip industry, is the introverted thinking sensation computer person. One of the most interesting people in this category was a young computer programmer whom I saw for many years. For the first five years of his therapy, he worked at his job, read philosophy, and smoked marijuana. Then he gradually stopped smoking marijuana, and analysis began in earnest. Almost all of his dreams would take him back to his hometown, where he would interact with members of his large Catholic family. A sharp introverted thinking type, he always wanted to *understand* these dreams, painstakingly working over each image. This process did enable him to come to a valuable intellectual understanding of his inner material. From my side, I would add the extraverted intuition to relate this material to his actual current life. Sharing these dreams and the work of interpreting them brough about a real connection between us, one that developed over the next few years into a sense of friendly collaboration. When he finally terminated, I felt that we had both made great strides in understanding and valuing a different perspective.

Regardless of psychological types the level of closeness a person can experience depends upon such factors as family dynamics, basic energy level, and the environmental setting. However, I do think that the type of person makes a big difference in how closeness is *experienced*. An extraverted intuitive feeling analyst such as myself can evoke, even provoke, closeness. My own natural response is to pick up on some nonverbal clues or dreams of the patient, and before either of us knows it, we are in vulnerable areas. Obviously, that is not necessarily a good thing because it overrides defenses. Often it would be much better if I could wait, be more introverted, and let the process develop more slowly. My natural way may be experienced as intrusive by the patient: sometimes I can feel the patient recoil as if being violated. Yet, many times my style of relating helps to break the ice and opens up important areas in therapy. I suspect there are similar positives and negatives to each type's approach to closeness.

A second important variable affecting the feeling of closeness in the analytical relationship has to do with self-disclosure on the part of the analyst. In the early days of analytical psychology (in contrast to psychoanalysis), self-disclosure was routine, as were extra-analytic relationships of various sorts with the analysand. The number of people involved in Jungian work then was small; the impact of the transference was not fully realized; and Jung had had a compensatory feeling reaction to the Freudian notion of the analyst as a blank screen. As time has passed and the schools of analysis have grown more similar to each other in theory and practice, extra-analytic contacts between patient and analyst in Jungian work have lessened dramatically. There has also been a shift among analytical psychologists in their attitudes toward self-disclosure in analysis.

We should try to say what we mean by self-disclosure. It means different things to different analysts. For instance, do we tell our patients where we are going on vacation? Do we tell them whether we are married or not, have

families, and so forth? These general forms of self-disclosure are certainly important, but they are not what I most
focus on when I think of self-disclosure. I am most concerned with situations when a patient has a particular
problem, for example a relationship issue, and the analyst
gives examples from his or her own life experience. At
such times, the analyst will be moved to share his or her
own life experience as an immediate way of helping the
patient to realize that he or she is not alone. Sharing that
the analyst has gone through a similar experience brings a
kind of intimacy or closeness that is dramatically immediate. We naturally would expect that there has been an
increased trend toward closeness in the analytical field.
There are, however, power aspects as well as relational
ones. If the analyst is older and the patient has a strong
parental projection, this sharing can be, and is, seen as the
voice of wisdom speaking to the less experienced, vulnerable patient, even an implicit suggestion that the patient
handle the situation as the analyst did. Despite the problems associated with fostering identifications, there is no
doubt that this type of self-disclosure can be of value to
the patient, and that it increases the bonding in the analytical relationship.

I'd like (with some trepidation) to give a recent example
from my own practice. A male patient in his late thirties
recently went through a divorce initiated by his wife; he
protested her decision to end their marriage all the way
through the process. For many months we discussed the
breakup and analyzed its meaning. One day when he was
feeling particularly down about his situation, I told him
about my own divorce some twenty-three years ago. I told
him what a difficult time it had been for me and that I
could understand the deeply felt pain he was suffering at
that moment. I knew he could see that I was feeling all

right now and that, basically, I had lived through the experience. I assured him that it was a most important experience for me. Although I would never have chosen it, it was a most important time, and I could even say, in retrospect, I was glad that it had happened. The overall effect was certainly to increase the closeness in the analytic relationship! He appreciated that I shared my experience with him, and it has subsequently felt fine to me to have spoken about it with him, although I have greater trepidation writing about it in this chapter.

One may ask what criteria I used to decide whether to tell him about my divorce. The main criterion I go by in such a decision is whether the issue is one on which I am still actively working or not. My divorce happened many years ago, and it has been an object of so much analysis and discussion over the years that I can probably claim to have metabolized it. At present, it does not pull on me very much, and I feel relatively free to talk about it. Were the issue still very much alive today, I would not have felt as free to speak about it and would most probably have kept silence. Often one may not be fully aware of how an issue is still working unconsciously in one, so that with a less "digested" issue, one can disclose material that one should not. I have found that the best guide is to follow one's own unconscious process, honoring a feeling of appropriateness, and to obtain consultation if there is a doubt.

Over the years, I have become aware of the dangers and pitfalls of self-disclosure so that I have become more reticent than I once was to share much in the way of personal material. This caution does not mean that I am any less there in the dialectic of the analysis, but it does mean that I am less apt to make my personal life a topic for discussion in analysis. I have learned from having said certain things about my life that later inhibited or affected patients' responses. Some have been unwilling to say certain thins for fear that they would hurt my feelings. They may know certain vulnerable areas of my life and will be afraid to talk about situations for fear that I will be sensitive. I have also seen other therapists and analysts who have been self-disclosing encourage their patients to live out a pattern that seems too close to the analyst's own. The patient's living out the same situation has validated the analyst's own life choices and also immortalized the analyst's pathology. In these cases, rather than there being an increased closeness, there was what Jung called *participation mystique*, an unconscious identification existing between the patient and the analyst. I think that self-disclosure is a tricky business in analysis, and I use it less and less in my practice, as unconsciousness so easily enters the situation. On the other hand, I do not rule it out as a therapeutic technique. Used judiciously, self-disclosure can foster a valuable connection, a therapeutic symbiosis, between patient and analyst.

We must now turn to a fuller treatment of the variable of *transference* in affecting closeness in the analytic relationship. The next example illustrates what can happen when a particular type of transference is accepted by both patient and analyst. The patient is a woman in her later thirties, divorced, with two small children. She became interested in Jung at the time of her marital breakup and began an analysis with me that had been going three years. Her relationships to men had been problematic, and she had alternated between being consumed by totally unavailable men or being totally alone. Most of the three years of her treatment, she had been alone. She was an attractive woman who got lots of attention from men, but she overwhelmed them with her needs. All her relationships to men had been eroticized, starting with her father. No actual incest had occurred, but there was a strong love/ hate bond between them. Toward her mother, she had a more distant, formal relationship. During the entire time of the analysis, she had been "in love" with her first psychology professor, who, after some initial seductive behavior, made it clear that he had no romantic interest in her. He was constantly in her fantasies. At the three-year mark of treatment, she had a dream that is a propos the topic of closeness. I paraphrase it. She dreamt that she was in her bedroom with me. It was night time and we were going to sleep. We were not lovers, and there were no sexual feelings. There was a good feeling of intimacy between us as we lay there talking. Many things happened in the dream, but then my wife began making lots of noise in the guest bedroom. I left to see what was happening, and my wife and daughter were in an argument. My daughter wanted to make a long-distance call, and there was some argument over it. The patient was for letting my daughter make her phone call. The dispute was settled, and I came back to bed with the patient. Later the patient's mother and sister came in for a while. She became angry at their intrusion, and the dream ended. The patient had a difficult time telling me this dream. To me, the basic message of the dream (and the reason for her discomfort) was that she felt *accepted* by me. I was in the father role in the dream, and genuine intimacy was expressed between us. There was expressly *no* sexual or erotic feeling present, which was quite different for this woman with her history of eroticized ambivalent relationships with men. She was not completely comfortable with the situation, but it remained constant throughout the dream. It was also all right for her to lie with me and exclude my wife and daughter for the moment. The dream has an obvious

Oedipal aspect in which she experiences the competition for attention with my wife as a mother object, and in which she won temporarily. Like many patients who equate transference with feelings of sexual arousal toward the therapist, she believed that she did not have a "transference toward me." I reassured her that the feelings she did have toward me were natural and accepted by me. She felt relieved by this interpretation and by our discussion of the dream, and there was a definite feeling of intimacy and closeness at the end of the session. I think the critical element in producing this increased closeness was not her transference to me per se, but that I *accepted* her transference in exactly the form it offered itself.

The vague word *closeness* conjures up many different images and feelings. It is easy to speculate but hard to pin down what the origins of all these feelings and images are. I have attempted primarily to talk not about transference as the basis of closeness, because that is a well-rehearsed area of analytic thought that can miss the crucial role of the analyst's real personality, attitudes, and behavior in creating, or squelching, a feeling of closeness. I have focused on two factors in myself, my psychological type and my attitude toward self-disclosure, which have either contributed to or taken away from the feeling of closeness I have been able to engender in the analytic relationship. Then I have discussed my acceptance of a patient's positive father transference toward me, an acceptance of her that enhanced the feeling of closeness in our work. In the background, however, has been the inevitable fact that my own patients have been looking to me to provide some sense of closeness in order to counteract a painful void in their own lives. I was sensitive to this need because it is an issue that affects us all.

Closeness and the Patient

Kendra Crossen

"Things that are real are given and received in silence."
—*Meher Baba*

Once a month

Twice a week I enter a room, close the door, and for 30 - fifty minutes sit opposite a man who smiles gently at me, looks steadily into my eyes, appears to be intently interested in everything I say, and doesn't complain if I tell him he's doing it all wrong. At last, someone who really understands me!

Too bad I can't really believe in that fantasy. I know that when my analyst nods empathically or affirms what I've said, it doesn't necessarily mean that he sees things my way or finds me uniquely fascinating. Such fantasies, I know, come from a desire for love. Because love is intimately connected with the deepest instincts of consciousness, I realize that I can find it without resorting to fantasy if I follow the principle "Don't look *for* love, look *at* it."

Although there are experiences of proximity between people that one would not characterize as love, I try to focus on love as the important ingredient in closeness, because that's where the healing energy is. I hope that when I experience moments of being close to this energy, my analyst does too, or at least has his own such moments.
priest
It's important to me to feel that we are equal recipients in

the relationship; otherwise I might have an uncomfortable sense of indebtedness. The ~~fee~~ ^thanks^ that I pay him I regard as compensation for his time, training, and experience; but how can ^even thanks^ money be a medium for the exchange of energy that takes place on the soul level?

I recognize the presence of love by the feelings of lightness, tranquillity, freedom, and expansion of being that it brings. In this presence there is no grasping desire, possessiveness, or narrowing of consciousness, although I may experience those things at other times.

Love is obviously not all warm, fuzzy communion. Self-restraint, courtesy, conscious effort, and the observation of boundaries are needed if love is to have a real and lasting value in any relationship. It feels good when it seems that we are practicing these disciplines together. As a result of the boundaries we observe, a space between us is created, a sacred emptiness in which any feeling, thought, image, or relationship may arise. Since we're not "out there" living them in the ordinary way, but are "in here" trying to be conscious of them, the situation presents a unique opportunity. Sometimes I imagine that we are like companions in meditation, trying to maintain our attention to the process no matter what comes up. Some of what comes up could evoke pain, anger, confusion, or excitement, which might capture our attention; but we can keep sitting, keep witnessing the play of phenomena in the empty space. Although we are talking during the session, I think that the real work takes place in silence, out of sight, sparked by the friction of opposites that arise from the contact between us.

Closeness does not require touching, but it does allow real contact. Eye contact can create a powerful flow of energy. There is also the sound of the voice, which can have a palpable effect. I once told my ~~analyst~~ ^priest^ that I felt as

46

So sorry for trying to push a point of vie re Past. Council t the office.

if I were going to be forced to tell something. I remember *feeling shame constricting my blood vessels.* the sensation of my back pressing tensely against the back of the couch. Now, ~~two years later~~ *three months later*, I can still experience a feeling of relaxation by recalling the sound of his voice when he said, "~~I'll never force you to do anything.~~" *Let's leave it behind & move ahead.*

I sometimes get caught in the friction between us or become hyperaware of the power imbalances. I'm a woman, he's a man. ~~I'm a Jew, he's a WASP.~~ I'm the *parishoner* ~~patient~~, he's the *Priest* ~~doctor~~. I tell him my stuff, he doesn't tell me his stuff. At other times I forget about my lower status and think that I'm light-years ahead of him. In either case, the feeling of separativeness is a barrier to closeness. Maybe it's a deliberate barrier, though, one that I contrive in order to preserve closeness by making sure there's not too much of it.

The best thing is to be close enough to maintain a bond but detached enough to keep the space open. But I don't want to try too hard to make sure the degree of closeness is exactly right, because control and manipulation are incompatible with love. The goal, I think, is not to worry about being close to ~~my analyst~~ *Fr. Steve* but to allow myself to draw close to that love of divine origin which not only heals all wounds but makes each of us, in our own individual way, true to ourselves and to others.

Dreams of an Analysand Dying of AIDS

Harry A. Wilmer

John was a forty-one-year-old sophisticated psychologist who was professionally dedicated to analytical psychology. He came to see me for analysis as part of his work as a candidate in a Jungian society. He had previously been in analysis with another Jungian analyst in Texas and had gone to San Francisco, where he had seen his second Jungian analyst. While he was in San Francisco, he developed a fever and thought he might have AIDS, but he put this thought out of his mind. He returned to Texas and began analysis with me. John was my analysand for three years before he was diagnosed as being HIV positive.

Several months before the diagnosis, he began experiencing fatigue, fever, and confusion in his business as a private practitioner. I recommended that he get a blood test to determine if he was HIV positive. He saw a gay physician who, to my astonishment, told him that he did not have AIDS and that the blood test was unnecessary. John was all too willing to accept this happy diagnosis, but his symptoms did not diminish.

Unmistakable symptoms associated with AIDS came upon John with devastating suddenness. Between Monday and Wednesday he became so weak that he could barely walk, and diffuse Kaposi's sarcoma lesions appeared over his body. By Thursday these tumors had spread to the soles of his feet and were so painful that he could only crawl across the floor. His arms were so weak that he could barely open the sliding glass patio door. He watched in dismay as his cat easily pushed open the door and slithered out.

He called me and described his symptoms: a sore throat, swollen glands, severe difficulty breathing. I arranged for him to be admitted to the university hospital to be cared for by the AIDS specialist there. The hospital adjoined the medical school, and I went to see him that afternoon. The diagnosis was established. By now, he was suffering from *pneumocystis carinii* pneumonia. He was on oxygen and had fluids running into each arm intravenously. He was in isolation, and as was the policy, I put on a gown, mask, and white cap before I went into the room. I was apprehensive because I had never seen "a case of AIDS" before. I must have been rather stiff, because several weeks later, John told me of his anger at me for being so "clinical," so unlike the kindly analyst in his comfortable office. But how could I have reacted any differently?

I recalled how in 1940 when I spent a year in a tuberculosis sanatorium, all my visitors wore masks because of TB's contagiousness and because at the time there were no drugs to treat the disease. I, like John, kept asking, "Why me?" But I said nothing of the *déjà vu* to him. Yet this was to be the initiation rite into a new relationship in which distance, closeness, and compassion took on new meaning.

> At that moment, when all the world around him melted away, when he stood alone like a star in the heavens, he was overwhelmed by a feeling of icy despair, but he was

more firmly himself than ever. That was the last shudder of his awakening, the last pains of his birth.[1]

Dream Series. Prior to his first hospitalization, John's dreams had been complex, long, and frequent. He generally viewed them in terms of their archetypal nature and mythology with which he was quite conversant. After his illness was diagnosed, the dreams changed. They became shorter, more clearly narrative, and less complex. They were like a seriatim of an archetypal journey of dying. The dreams were in no way AIDS-specific, and it would be foolish to have imagined that they were, or to make an arbitrary construct. Rather they represented the symbolic way in which the unconscious psyche copes with a death sentence and the inexorable destruction of the mind and body. The "death sentence" was not psychologically processed like a catastrophic trauma, but it was as if some mysterious messenger had confirmed a feeling with a prophetic message. I came to think of the dreams as if they were words from Tiresius, the blind seer or prophet who was noted for his androgynous wisdom. Tiresius mediated between the worlds of the living and the dead. The dead who crossed into the mythological underworld drank of the River Styx and lost their memory; Tiresius alone among the shades retained his memory and intelligence, and brought messages from the dead to the upper world. He had the power of interpreting dreams.

When John was discharged from the hospital, he continued his analytic hours with me at my office. At first I was uneasy, wondering what my patients would think once they knew he had AIDS. Would they stop coming to see me? But his sessions with me and his dreams in particular were a central bond that held us close and that, in the hallucinatory imagery of the dream world, offered meaning and psychological healing to his suffering and, in the end, to his peaceful death. His shorter, more precise and memorable dreams helped him cope with his sense of inferiority, shame, mourning, helplessness, isolation, rejection, and a shattered self-image. He was, of course, depressed, but that diminished dramatically without any medication.

Three nights before his hospitalization, he reported the following dream to me:

> I am running down a football field, and the ball is thrown to me. I can see it sail through the air and I catch it and run for a touchdown. Then I realize that there is no opposing team, and no one in the stadium.

John commented, "Don't you think that is a strange dream?" Answering himself before I could say a word, he added, "I suppose it means that I am going in the proper direction." To me it had a more somber meaning. There was no resistance, and there seemed to be no purpose to the touchdown, and against whom was he playing? Did catching something relate to the AIDS? It was not a dream of a hero, and no one was in the stadium to cheer him on. Is it too farfetched to think that the resistance (i.e., antibody) was deficient and that the game and score were pointless? But is it not then likely that the very pointlessness and meaninglessness explained the dream's deeper message—that his heretofore ambitious drive for achievement, recognition, and accomplishment in the outer world was really insignificant and that he no longer had to strive for fame and glory? It made no point. Now facing death, his drive was of a deeper kind and his efforts had to be made alone. While there might be temporary periods of recovery, the only real healing was in his psyche in *vis medicatrix naturae,* the healing power of nature, of himself.

It was this inner physician who would speak through the voice of the dream and his creative imagination. He began painting and writing poetry. Since he no longer could manage his private practice, he began counseling AIDS patients through the San Antonio AIDS foundation. He brought me many poems. Here are two:

> My hands have difficulty
> curving the words
> spoken from the heart
> where all that is true
> emerges from
> suffering's gentle embrace.

And:

> Fear and love have
> been constant visitors
> like calls from some
> distant place. My
> body foreign, my heart
> strong, a familiar
> companion and guide.

Two nights before his hospitalization, John dreamed:

I am in the background watching a flying saucer. There are hundreds of people in it, perhaps over three hundred. There is a sense of levity and adventure. The saucer is setting down on the earth. In the middle of all the people, a woman is standing in a very bright light focused on her.

John noted, "I am still earthbound, but maybe it's a sort of background to eternity. It is like a mandala, and perhaps the Great Mother stands in a beam of light." Then he reflected on the previous dream, saying, "Do you think the long pass is like a long passing, like death?"

The feeling tone in my office during John's sessions was intense. We shook hands when he departed, and once in a while I would put my hand on his shoulder as he left. In the two months after discharge from hospital, he was given chemotherapy and radiation therapy and grew weak, gaunt, and pale. He was contemplating stopping the radiation and chemotherapy because of the side effects and his sometimes troubled thinking. Although he told me many dreams, the one he told me after he had been out of the hospital for two months was particularly important because of the transference significance.

> I am in a class for seniors in a four-year college. The course being taught was on religion and the philosophy of life. It was taught by a Franciscan nun whom I recognized as my actual first-grade teacher.

He told me, "I woke up at this point and then went to sleep again and continued dreaming."

> I am in Tibet. I am teaching a course in religion and philosophy of life. I see a woman who I know is my wife, but in the dream I am going to marry her. When we are married, she will be the queen and I will be the king. We are dressed in richly embroidered Tibetan garments. Then I begin trimming my beard, knowing that I would be meeting my mother, and it would please her.

John's mother had died one year before the clinical appearance of his AIDS, so the reunion would be with his dead mother. He is preparing to graduate from college, and his teacher is the same one who instructed him in the beginning of his education. The Franciscan order indicates poverty, service, simplicity, and humility, relinquishing all the outer trimmings and trappings of the material world of competition.

The stages in his dreams developed from the competitive ambitious run in the football stadium to graduation to a new beginning with the anticipation of meeting his dead mother. The new beginning is symbolically portrayed in the Tibetan royal marriage scene. Tibet is associated with Buddhism and religious mysticism, as well as with *The Tibetan Book of the Dead,* for which Jung had written an important psychological commentary.[2] At the time of John's dream, Tibet was a country being destroyed by the Chinese invaders, its monasteries and religious artifacts ruined, its monks killed, and its works burned. Tibet is a poor but more materialistic world than the Franciscan order. In a way, to be a king dressed in beautiful clothes is an inflation. The symbolic wedding, in the dreams of dying people, often represents a marriage with the other part of one's personality, a completeness, as if it were a cosmic unity that existed before us and into which we are preparing to enter.

Marie-Louise von Franz noted that many dying people are known to have the mystical marriage or love experience, resulting in the tradition that death is a kind of mystical marriage with the other half of the personality.[3] Jung wrote that the alchemical wedding is a Western equivalent of the fundamental principle of the Chinese union of yang and yin in the Tao, and that the consummation of the *mysterium coniunctionis* is the unity of spirit, soul, and body made one with the original *unus mundus.* In alchemy, this drama is enacted by the King and Queen.[4]

It is important to note that John and I had long ago spoken of Tibetan Buddhism in relation to a dream. It is my custom to advise my patients ahead of time when I will be away for any long period. Four months previously,

I had told him that I was going to take a trip to Lhasa, Tibet. The day after I had told him of my plan to go to Tibet, he dreamed that *he* was going to Tibet. When he related this dream, almost without thinking, I instantly said, "John, you will probably get there before me." He said nothing but was silent for a long time. Later I had to cancel this trip to Tibet. Because of some angina associated with effort, my doctor told me not to take this trip because I would be driving over a pass seventeen thousand feet high. When John told this second dream about being in Tibet (above), he commented, "You know, Harry, what you said before about my getting to Tibet before you was one of the most important things you ever said to me. It was a humane way of saying something, and many times since then it has come back to comfort me."

John began to be disturbed by memory lapses that he regarded as a sign of beginning dementia. Two of John's friends had just died of AIDS with dementia. His symptoms forced him to stop working. Since he could no longer earn money, he moved into a cheaper apartment. He told me this dream:

> I am standing in a lavishly furnished apartment on the top floor, about twenty or thirty floors up. The windows reach from floor to ceiling and there is an amazing all-around view. On one side are the woods and on the other is the city. It is remarkable how clear everything is. I am arranging a reception because I am going to get married, and after the ceremony we are going to take a trip.
>
> The same night I had a second dream in which I am attending a training seminar in a Jungian society where the spiritual side seems to be neglected. A male training analyst says, "This should teach you the lesson of alchemy."

In the first part of the dream, John is living in luxury—
a far cry from the Franciscan poverty. From his elevated
position, he can see a sweep of nature and civilization. He
can see it with remarkable clarity. He is above it all. The
materialistic finery, like the elegant Tibetan clothes, is
perhaps not only inflation, and being high, but also compensation for his lowly status and near poverty. The second part of the dream is a learning situation. Now we hear
the voice of the unconscious pronouncing the alchemical
(death) wedding and the journey. The male training analyst is *not* me, though he projects his inner analyst onto
me. For me to interpret him as myself would be a narcissistic, inflated intrusion into the dream. It is not me, it is
his inner guru.

John expressed his reaction in a poem:

Ancient stones
moaning across the green fields
memories growing,
some flowering
shed a crystalline light.

Three weeks before his death, he told me this dream:

I dive into a swimming pool. As I go down, I look to
the left side of the pool, and on the stone side of the
pool is a stick drawing of a shaman in an ancient cave.
The shaman has green, yellow, and red feathers around
his neck, wrists, and ankles. As I sink further down, I
suddenly find myself in a bright light. I struggle, swimming upward, and I hear a man's voice, "If you follow
the light, the light will, of its own accord, carry you to
the end of your journey."

Sinking into the darkness of the night, or water, appears
in many dying people's dreams, and the paradoxical appearance of light from the depth also characterizes such

dream experiences. The struggle to come up is followed by the voice that tells him to follow the light (down) and that this will lead him to the end of this life and death journey.

This is the last dream John told me before he died:

> I am with a woman, my soul woman. I have a key to my house in the country, and when I see the light in this dream I know I have AIDS and that it was a part of me, and that I was myself in every way. It was like going home, and I felt good.

The key to his house in the country is "ancient stones moaning across the green fields" where he was going home to live in peace—"memories growing, some flowering" and the illumination "shed a crystalline light."

John had refused to continue his radiation and chemotherapy treatment though he was the first person in San Antonio to be given one of the AIDS-specific drugs. He had once been admitted to the emergency room in acute respiratory failure, and I met him there. I placed my hand on his abdomen and stroked it once or twice as I would have done with a suffering child. This closeness between us was far different now from the day I visited him the first time he was hospitalized.

John was admitted to the hospital a week before his death, and against his wishes was placed on intubation, intravenous feeding, and oxygen. I saw him before he died.

He was semiconscious, and his father and sister had come from out of town to be with him. Before I left I wanted to say something very personal to him. Despite the presence of his family in the room, I moved near him and whispered into his ear, "John, follow the light." He nodded and was silent. He died peacefully in his bed at home two days later, just as he had wanted.

It was, perhaps, a fulfillment of the orphic hymn to Aesclepius, god of medicine, "Come blessed one, helper, to give life a noble ending."

I had been planning to present a public education program on AIDS at the University of Texas Health Science Center medical school at San Antonio, where I would show a video tape (which included John) on the subject. The project, called "The Inner World of AIDS: A Confrontation," consisted of edited teaching tapes and a manual from fifteen hours of video-taped sessions of two groups of health-care workers and AIDS patients focusing on the emotion and feeling responses of both patient and caretaker.

My own acceptance of and bond with John was revealed to me a few weeks before his death when I was to present a program on AIDS as part of grand rounds for the psychiatric department of the University of Texas Health Science Center. My presentation would include the video tape with John speaking to a group of mental health workers.

As the time for grand rounds approached, John lay dying in the university hospital. I visited him on my morning rounds that day to tell him about grand rounds. I placed one hand on his arm as if to reach him more easily. When I told him that the subject of my talk would be AIDS and that the video tape we had made would be shown, he was happy. He wanted to tell me something, he said, and asked me to write it down since he was too weak to hold a pen. This is what he dictated:

> I wish [you would] use my name in the video tape we made to help change the attitude toward the disease

which touches all sectors of human life. Hopefully the
tape can change the attitude of the average American.

NOTES

1. Hermann Hesse, *Siddhartha* (New York: New Directions,
   1951), p. 34.
2. C. G. Jung, "Psychological Commentary," in *The Tibetan
   Book of the Dead, or the After-Death Experiences on the Bardo
   Plane,* 2nd ed., ed. W. Y. Evans-Wentz (New York: Oxford
   University Press, 1960).
3. Marie-Louise von Franz, *Alchemy: An Introduction to the Symbolism and the Psychology* (Toronto: Inner City Books, 1980),
   p. 179.
4. Jung, *Mysterium Coniunctionis,* CW, 17, pp. 463–464.

Inner Dialogue of Patient and Analyst

A Poem by Carol A. Mouché

C arol A. Mouché, now the editor of a prize-winning national magazine and the winner of awards for writing and photography, sought psychotherapy when she was in her teens. Sensitive to the stigma of being labeled "mentally unbalanced," she has been energetic in helping people to see that seeking psychological help when they need it is a sign not of weakness but of strength. When she was Associate Editor at the Institute for the Humanities at Salado, after typing a paper of mine on the inner dialogue of analyst and patient, she brought me the following poem, which she had written many years ago during her psychotherapy for depression. The poem dramatically conveys her feelings about her inner, unspoken dialogue. She hopes that it might help other patients *and* therapists to realize the importance of such inner, silent closeness, by making them conscious of what the mind is doing. When a doctor is not aware of a patient's inner speech but is only aware of his or her own inner dialogue, the result may well be an inflation in the therapist. When a patient writes out such inner dialogues, there is a creative drama that evokes insight and fosters self-healing through an understanding of closeness and distance.—H.A.W.

Carol A. Mouché

(Don't leave the cage-door open)

Why must it be kept quiet when
    (Don't leave the cage-door open, the monkeys)
I'm not the only one who
    (like to run out but they don't)
Feels this way?
    (always like to come back.)
So I talk to professionals
    (The zoologists want to observe this)
In another attempt to refine
    (rare species, because their traits)
My ideas. Sometimes it
    (are peculiar to this climate, and)
Works, sometimes it doesn't but
    (these monkeys aren't quite as intelligent)
Most of the time I feel like
    (as we'd like them to be.)
I'm not communicating.
    (I think they understand us)
Do you understand?
    (so, don't leave the cage-door open.)

                Carol A. Mouché (1978)

The Boundary-Maker in Relationships of Closeness and Trust

Peter Rutter

In Europe, he is called Hermes, Mercurius, and Loki. In North America, he is Coyote. The world over, he appears in every single psychotherapy hour, in every psychotherapist's and client's psyche, every day. Hermes-Coyote may be a trickster, but he is also the guardian of the boundary. He *is* the boundary, and he is the boundary-maker. This is the very boundary which, elaborated over physical and psychological space, generates a container, a vessel, a *temenos*. Only within the intact, bounded *Hermetic* container can a healing relationship occur. Without having Hermes-Coyote on your side, without a good and reasonably conscious relationship with your shape-shifting boundary-maker, you will not heal. You will destroy and be destroyed.

What does it mean to have a developed relationship with your boundary-maker, to have Hermes-Coyote on your side? To answer that, first let us carefully examine what it means when he is *not* on your side, when instead he tricks you, and, through your own unconscious, renders the boundaries so shifty, so indiscriminate, that you lose control over them. Let us identify and then confront the ways in which all of us in the healing, pastoral, teaching, and mentoring professions can be destructive within the very relationships of closeness and trust that our professional titles guarantee us.

Let us look at the destructive side first, not with the illusion that we can, by the simple process of elimination, identify and sequester off the bad in hopes that the remainder will be the good. Instead, let us face the destructive side with some faith that we will be changed in the process.

I do not mean to be presumptuous in asking that we be changed. You might think that because you have held to a high ethical standard concerning boundaries, I should be asking those with lower ethical standards, not you, to change. But I am not focusing here on those who are not in good relation to Coyote, who are not favored with good and ethical boundaries. If we really want to stop the enormous tide of destructive acts committed by those of us in the helping professions, we must *all* change. The burden of such a task inescapably falls most heavily on the *most* ethical. It is precisely because the less ethical among us are who they are that the burden—and honor—of providing ethical leadership falls upon the more ethical. They are best equipped to provide it.

Discussion of the ways in which a poor relationship with our own boundary-maker makes us destructive begins with the word *exploitation,* which my dictionary defines as "selfish employment for one's own use or advantage." Relationships of closeness and trust mandate that we guard and promote the interests of the client, parishioner, student, or protegé. By definition, exploitation involves the *abandonment* of the interests of the other in favor of one's own interests.

Although there are, sadly, countless forms of exploitative abandonment, it is the sexual form, with its severe damage, that has become so overwhelmingly visible. Because sexual exploitation involves an irrevocable physical act, it offers concrete evidence of a boundary that has also been violated invisibly and psychologically. And because a preponderance of cases involve a man in power who sexually exploits a woman, the relationship of trust is a microcosm of the many ways that values relating to boundaries, trust, and closeness have become corrupted in our larger society, a phenomenon I have elsewhere referred to as "sex in the forbidden zone."[1]

We must extrapolate from the physical act of sexual exploitation of trust the less visible psychological damage we may cause our patients, clients, and students. In perceiving the damage at this more subtle level, we should then be able to recognize the earliest forms of exploitation in ourselves or in our colleagues and act to prevent it.

Explicitly broadening the field of scrutiny beyond ourselves to include our colleagues is absolutely critical to the development of an ethical atmosphere in the professions. Ethics, after all, are collective standards as well as personal ones, and those of us who value individual autonomy must understand and act against collective forces that destroy individuals either one by one or en masse. When we experience how the trickster becomes the destroyer, we inevitably recognize that it is not enough merely to ensure one's own good boundaries. We must also now negotiate another boundary: the one that reaches beyond our own behavior to our judging, and at times speaking up about, the behavior of our colleagues.

When we examine, in its earliest, nascent stages, destructive behavior in relationships of closeness and trust, we may at first uncover something human and at times unavoidable: inattentiveness to the other. You sit in your chair, in session with a client, and gradually you notice that you are not keeping your thoughts on your client. The boundaries in your own psychic process are becoming skewed. Although you most assuredly need to continue having your own thoughts, the question becomes one of what value these thoughts have for the task at hand, which is to serve the interest of your client. At best, your intrapsychic boundary remains fairly permeable to upwellings of less conscious associations you may have to your client. But boundaries become skewed when the material that invades takes you further and further from your client. This does not become unethical or destructive every time it happens, but only when it remains persistent, progressive, and unremedied.

If you remain passive in the face of this inner boundary disturbance, you begin to go down the path to exploitative boundary violation of your client. To correct the inattention, try to redraw the boundary actively, either by your own inner examination, or with the help of your own therapist, supervisor, or consultant. One way to think of it is that you must, among other things, ask your own boundary-regulator, your own Hermes or Coyote, why he/she/it is disturbing your boundaries. The inattentiveness itself is not unethical; the failure to correct it is. If it persists, you are cheating the client out of the legitimate degree of close attention to his or her interests that he or she deserves. What is more, you are exploiting his or her presence with you, as well as the fee paid to you.

When you notice such a skew in yourself and then investigate the countertransference that is creating this inner boundary disturbance, you open the way to developing an even stronger conscious relationship with your Coyote, your boundary-maker. Once this inner relationship is begun, it can prepare you to deal with the elements of your own shadow that you will discover. Even if some of what you find in yourself is ostensibly destructive, if you contain it well, the destructive expression may be prevented. You may, for instance, find that in some way you don't care at all about this client; that you have some hatred or envy toward him or her; that you want this person to help you; that you want this person to give you a great deal of money or otherwise become a vehicle for you to become wealthy, admired, or less lonely; that you want to get much closer to this person in a way that disregards what he or she may need; that you are having sexual fantasies about this person; or, as a wholly separate mind-state from having fantasies, you find you very much want to touch your client sexually.

The intrapsychic distinction, the boundary, between having fantasies about a client and actually wanting to touch him or her is subtle yet critical. The ability to distinguish between them and to stay on the fantasy side of the boundary line is a critical indicator of how well developed one's relationship with one's boundary-maker has become. Realizing this distinction would involve the capacity to accept one's fantasies about a client and also feel somewhat sickened, or pained, rather than excited, about the prospect of actually touching him or her. But stealing pieces of who one's clients are or who one fantasizes them to be, either visually or psychologically, and using these pieces for one's own psychic means, has a different configuration entirely. This kind of inner boundary-crossing, which can start with deliberate inattention, or a persistent and conscious decision to steer one's thoughts away from the person in the room, lacks innocence from the beginning and is much more likely to lead to outer and visible destructiveness that the client will surely come to experience. Noticing this kind of nascent exploitation in oneself should lead to careful and deliberate reexamination of one's inner container to discover not only where the boundary-maker has gone, but where one's heart for the work may be hiding.

We can identify many paradigmatic issues of inner and outer boundary-making by examining nothing more than the unavoidable phenomenon of occasional inattention, without having to name specific acts toward our clients that might escalate from inattention to include insensitivity, cruelty, deception, punishment, or seduction. Any of these more intensified acts may lurk beneath a momentary inattention. On the other hand, each of these destructive impulses may arise on its own, fully formed, directly out of our psyches, and break past our inner boundaries to affect the client.

The ability to identify a nascent internal boundary problem allows us to work on it in a completely inner way, before it becomes an act that damages the client. This ability, this primary boundary-making that allows intrapsychic containment of our own psychic contents, is what all therapists must strive for in the service of their clients. The relative constancy of the therapist's inner boundary is perhaps the most important quality of all in determining whether a clinician can practice both competently and ethically. I strongly believe that such a quality is also central to ethical practice of other professions that involve closeness and trust between two people, even when practitioners of those professions do not customarily think in terms of transference and countertransference and psychological boundaries. These include clergy and spiritual leaders, lawyers, teachers, workplace mentors, and healers and helpers in all nonpsychologically oriented fields, including medicine, dentistry, chiropractic, acupuncture, physical therapy, optometry, podiatry, and beyond.

Let us direct our attention for a moment away from ourselves to the other person in the room: the client, the patient, the student, the parishioner, the protegé, and move beyond our internal boundaries to attend the boundary between ourselves and the other. Because we are the helping professionals, we are responsible not only for knowing how we form and regulate this boundary from our side, but also for knowing something about how boundary issues are experienced from the point of view of the other person who is looking back at us.

We must not underestimate how different we will look to the client when we are working in a healthy and responsible way with our own inner boundaries, as opposed to when we are not. You, as well as the boundary between the two of you, are critically important to your client, who is monitoring, perceptibly and imperceptibly, any nuance of your own inner boundary-making. Even when your struggle remains invisible, at some level the other person is looking to see whether he or she is safe with you, and whether what you do with your boundaries is going to upset or challenge his or hers.

At another level, usually unconsciously but possibly most meaningfully, the person you are there to help is trying hard to get some idea of how you maintain your inner boundaries. Whatever other kind of work you may be doing together, in the end what might be most important to this person is whether he or she can learn just a little from you about how to develop a healthier relationship with his or her inner boundary-maker. The client will learn not so much from what you *say* about boundaries (although this can be quite important) as from how you actually *are* about boundaries.

At best, the boundaries will allow psychological containment and productive integration of the enormous richness going on within each person, as well as between them, in a relationship based on closeness and trust. But because we cannot always be at our best, we must also be prepared to handle occasions when the intrapsychic boundary fails, when Coyote incites us to act in ways that the client can visibly perceive. What then? Once something visible has broken through—an insensitive or hurtful or selfish or inappropriately intimate comment, gesture, or act—our boundary-maker has an even greater challenge. Not only do we now need to work on our inner boundary, but simultaneously the boundary with the other requires repair. To complicate matters, the other may have alerted us to our lack of containment. We may not have noticed anything amiss in ourselves or in our relationship with the other until he or she began behaving differently toward us, or, if we have been fortunate, actually came right out and told us that he or she had problems with something we said or did.

The issue I am discussing is not the familiar clinical event in which the other misperceives, misinterprets, or, as part of the transference, otherwise distorts something the therapist has done. Rather it is when the therapist has actually allowed some inappropriate boundary behavior to occur. We need to be scrupulously honest with ourselves and admit to our own trickster-shadow behavior, rather than continue to blame clients and transference distortions, real or not. Such honesty develops in our own inner work as we continue to refine our relationship with the inner boundary-maker.

It takes extraordinary honesty to repair the boundary with the other regardless of who first noticed the disturbance. Once we accept the disturbance as a real event, not imagined by the client, it becomes our duty to allow the other to know it as a real event. Otherwise the other will have no way to understand and recover from his or her own resultant boundary disturbance. Remember that when you are in the room as a clinician, your own recovery of good boundaries may be fundamental to the entire process. Nevertheless the ultimate purpose of that effort is primarily to serve the development of healthier boundaries in the client.

Unless you can allow what emanated from you as a boundary disturbance to become real to the other, he or she will be trapped by the typical sort of psychological duplicity that is so rife in all of our psyches from messages we have all heard as we were growing up. These messages come implicitly and explicitly from within our families or from the social order in which we live. They tell us not to believe what we feel. Such messages devalue our intuitive relationship to the boundary-maker, which endows us with a built-in capacity to sense boundary disturbances with a high degree of subtlety. But when our perceptions of what is actually occurring at the boundary threaten the family or the social order, we are encouraged to turn against and devalue ourselves and our capacity to know the truth about what is happening at the boundary.

"We" refers to both therapist and client in this context because I do not think there is any meaningful difference in the degree to which the class of therapists and class of clients are afflicted by familial and cultural conspiracies to deny the truth of what is occurring at the intimate, inter-personal boundary. The client is likely to be more immediately symptomatic about boundary issues, but we professionals really need to admit that we, too, can become pathologically symptomatic at any time. We make this admission to one another in the professional literature, at conferences, and in ethical tribunals. But we need most of all to admit this to the client within the relationship of trust if we are to help him or her, and ourselves, reverse the process of devaluation of the individual that occurs when we deny the truth of what is going on at the boundary.

This brings us to the moment that may well make the difference, beyond anything else we do, for those we are charged with helping: the moment in which we will either ignore our own boundary lapse or allow the other to have the truth. Such moments challenge us on many levels. Will we be able to step beyond our own comfort, or step outside a professional ideology that reenacts in many respects the most dysfunctional ways family and social systems devalue the perceptions of the client? Here the client is the symbolic child to us as a symbolic parent, with our tendency to maintain traditional authority. Despite this, when a client questions something we have done, or when we notice in ourselves even a subtle boundary violation, will we be able to say, "I'm sorry. I shouldn't have said that to you. I shouldn't have treated you that way. The fact that I did so is my problem, not yours"?

To say such a thing to a client, when it represents a commitment to validating his or her experience of our skewed boundaries, can begin to revolutionize his or her relationship to the boundary-maker. It may be the first time in a relationship of closeness and trust that a person with a parental quality of authority has ever claimed responsibility for his or her own capacity to wound another through a boundary violation. It begins to free the client from a world where his or her perceptions have been, over time, systematically devalued.

At the same time, such an experience offers a new model for the client in his or her own life that may help interrupt the heritage of abuse that the abused pass on to those close to them. Despite my focus on the client as victim of our boundary problems, there is no doubt that when our clients lose control of their boundaries, they often victimize not only themselves, but also those to whom they are close. When they can experience us as symbolic parents with the courage to do something they thought impossible, the child in them is released from a seemingly perpetual trap, while the adult in our clients can identify with the parent-adult in us who has shown them a healthier realtionship with our boundary-maker.

I want to comment on the old caveat that we cannot expect these changes to occur overnight—that they need years of testing and working through in the therapeutic relationship. I have instead found that at times, you do see a change overnight when you treat a patient with unexpected honesty. Certainly any of us, professionals or clients, need years to reshape fundamental elements in our character. But when you change some of the fundamental rules of boundary behavior in relationships of closeness and trust, and change them in ways that deliver rarely spoken truths, sometimes you can see a sudden, quantum change in a client.

For instance, a client had a strong erotic transference to me that was manifested both in her dreams and in her consciously expressed wish that we become lovers. Over several weeks, I asked her to tell me more and more about these dreams and fantasies, a perfectly defensible psychotherapeutic strategy. One day, I suddenly realized that my Coyote was tricking me. I had crossed over a subtle inner boundary and was beginning to accept her erotic material more because it fascinated me than because I thought it was therapeutic for her to share it with me. My disturbed relationship to my boundary-maker was affecting her, I was sure, by pushing her dangerously farther from her already tenuous relationship with her own boundary-maker, a process that in the past had caused her to be sexually exploited because she had lost control of her sexual boundaries. That scenario was being repeated between us by my inciting her to continue providing me with her erotic fantasies.

Eventually, instead of responding to my patient's erotic fantasies by asking her to tell me more, I *became* the boundary-maker. I told her, for the first time, that the fact of my being her therapist precluded the possibility that we could ever have any sexual contact. I went on to say that I should have told her this sooner, but had delayed because her dreams and fantasies about the two of us having erotic contact had aroused a degree of fantasy in myself. No further explanation or detail was requested or necessary— in fact, any elaboration on my part would have constituted a new boundary violation.

For another patient such an intervention may have been terribly anxiety-provoking. It could have been perceived as invasive or might have seduced someone away from her own material into a curiosity about my fantasies. Yet the evidence from this patient's conscious behavior and unconscious content suggests that what I told her was deeply calming. In our very next session, she told me a dream in which she felt she was my daughter. This signaled a new and enduring element in her dream life and in our conscious relationship that was to last the duration of our work together. Once I *became* the father by explicitly telling her where my boundaries were, she could, in the transference, become the daughter. Her erotic dreams and fantasies about me stopped virtually overnight. I do not think this change would have occurred if I had not also accounted for the period when I was violating her boundaries by not being so careful about my own. If I had not told her about my boundary disturbance, I could have continued to be the boundary-maker for both of us. But by giving her a glimpse into my own boundary-making process, I also provided a way for her to become more conscious about her own.

Giving our clients this glimpse into our own struggles with boundary issues can have an unexpected healing impact because, among other things, it is a form of revealing the incest secret. We rarely acknowledge the degree to which we are codependent with our clients. But we do depend on them: for money, for company, for inspiration, for psychological growth, for sexual fantasy, and to some degree for self-validation. The degree of intimacy available to us through our clients inevitably awakens in us conflicted issues of closeness and kinship, and incest themes are part of any perception of kinship. By incest themes, I mean the constant consideration, whenever there is any closeness, of the question of how close we want to, need to, can or should get to the other person. A healthy answer to this question depends on our developing a relationship with our boundary-maker. When the occasion asks it of us, simply telling others that we struggle with our own boundaries lifts a significant part of the burden of dealing with the incest problem from the shoulders of those who have never had the opportunity to solve their own boundary problems. It is these people whom we should least of all enlist to help us solve ours.

I have personified the boundary-maker as Coyote, or as Hermes, Mercurius, and Loki, not to urge you to accept any particular psychological model, but to express the point that a perception of the location and quality of the boundary is possible in a palpable, real-life way at every moment we are interacting with another human being. I hope that through this personification of the boundary-maker, we might all become less passive about repairing boundary violations and work actively toward maintaining ethical and healthy boundaries that honor the self even as they honor the other. Such work can be done creatively and dynamically in every relationship in our lives: within ourselves, perceptibly and imperceptibly with the person sitting across the room, with our colleagues as individuals and in professional organizations, with our society and, finally, with the earth itself—where, by the way, Coyote still lives.

NOTE

1. Peter Rutter, *Sex in the Forbidden Zone: When Men in Power—Therapists, Doctors, Clergy, Teachers, and Others—Betray Women's Trust* (Los Angeles: Jeremy P. Tarcher, 1989; New York: Fawcett Books, 1991, paperback).

Confidentiality and Betrayal in the Therapy of Anne Sexton

A Dialogue with Diane Wood Middlebrook

Harry A. Wilmer

Diane Wood Middlebrook, the author of *Anne Sexton: A Biography,*[1] gave a seminar at the Institute for the Humanities at Salado, Texas, on April 6, 1991. Issues of closeness and intimacy dominated her presentation, titled "You Taught Me to Dream: The Story of Anne Sexton." The dream that Middlebrook spoke of was the fairy-tale life of Anne Sexton—suicidal housewife magically transformed into untouchable poet. The closeness that Middlebrook spoke of was between Sexton, seeking an escape from failed attempts at "normalcy," and her psychiatrist, Dr. Martin Orne, who first encouraged her to write. Sexual intimacy later developed between Sexton, now a successful poet, and a second psychiatrist. Both this closeness and this intimacy were designed to help keep the fairy tale going—but their reality is grim.

At the Salado seminar, five months before the publication of Sexton's biography, Middlebrook briefly alluded to the fact that she had acquired clinical records and three hundred audio tapes of Sexton's therapy sessions with Dr. Orne ten years before her suicide in 1974. Being a psychiatrist myself, I raised the question concerning the ethical foundation of a psychiatrist who would turn over such private material. This was a question that was repeatedly asked by others once the book was published. The *New York Times* first raised the issue with a front-page feature article on Middlebrook's book and the behavior of Dr. Orne. After that there followed a virtual avalanche of articles and letters in newspapers and magazines.

While the reviews of Middlebrook's book in these publications are consistently positive, the behavior of Dr. Orne is soundly criticized. Various accounts of his behavior have been uncovered, but it is interesting to note Middlebrook's own words at the Salado seminar on how she acquired this private and privileged material.[2]

WILMER: Would you say a word about the significance of listening to the taped interviews? Were these interviews that she taped or the doctor taped of the therapy?

MIDDLEBROOK: As I mentioned to you, Martin Orne cooperated with me by giving me an interview in 1985 after I had been working on the book for about five years. In fact, I had written up parts of it, including an account of Sexton's treatment by him. He agreed to an interview, which is unusual. The psychiatrists said on the whole that they couldn't break confidentiality. He was persuaded by some of my colleagues at Stanford who knew him quite well to help me out. So we had an interview at which both of us were quite emotional as we were thinking about her. And I think impulsively, in fact, at that interview he decided to let me listen to the tapes of the therapy sessions that he had made with her. Now, I knew about these tapes. Let me tell you the reason that he was treating her by taping her.

Around the time of her mother's death, Sexton, in

1959, had developed a symptom during her therapy session. She would go into what she called trances that were self-induced hypnotic states. She had been hypnotized when she was having her jaws worked on. She knew how to put herself under hypnosis, actually, and her doctor was a person who specialized in hypnosis, so the hypnosis state was one that she was familiar with. She began going into these [states] during therapy hours, and when they were over she wouldn't be able to wake up. Very often he would have to bring her out of the trance by counting as if she were under hypnosis. In addition, she would have no memory of what happened in the session. This was an extremely retarding kind of thing to go on in the therapy. He tried to treat it as a symptom, but it went on for a year. So, he said, "We've got to do something about this. We are stalled here. I want you to do this. I want you after every session to try to make notes about what has gone on in the session." But she wouldn't be able to remember anything, literally. So he decided to start taping her. He said to me, "She was making *me* into her memory. I wanted *her* to be the one who possessed her memories. So I suggested that we tape the sessions and that she make notes after each session about what she remembered and then listen to the tapes and take notes about that." So . . . not only would she encounter herself in this process, but she would have a way of capturing or getting the memory.

This was a very successful kind of treatment. She began to do much better. It went on until 1964 when [Dr. Orne] was offered a job at the University of Pennsylvania and left Boston. She entered treatment with another doctor. So the tapes start January 1961 [and continue] through 1964, three times a week, except when her doctor was on vacation. She would be taped and then would make these notes. The estate had permitted me to read the notes that she had made, which were at the University of Texas library under restriction.[3] They decided that I could see anything, so I followed the Anne Sexton annotations, which are hard to read. I pulled a lot of stuff out of them, but what I wanted when I went to talk to Dr. Orne was, "Did I get this right? Do I understand this?" They were muddled sort of shorthand notes that she made. Well, I was asking questions, and he would say, "I can't really remember the answer to that because I don't know. I just really can't remember." So he said, "I don't see why, since the family decided that you could see this notebook, you shouldn't hear the tapes as well, since those are the sources of Sexton's notes."

Now, this was at the end of this interview, and I was astounded first of all that the tapes existed, and secondly that he was willing to let me hear them. However, he did not *act* impulsively. About fourteen months passed before he actually sent them to me. I thought that he had thought better of it. I didn't tell anybody except my husband that he said this to me. I wondered if he really would [let me hear the tapes]. I thought he would be like anybody else and fall into the bewitchment of the interview and later wake up and say, "Wait a minute, this is not a good idea. What have I done?" He later explained that he felt he had to discuss the matter with colleagues; he also wished to establish procedures for my use of quotations from them in the book.

Once I had actually gotten them, and gotten the material in a state that I could at least consult, I began to talk to psychiatrists about how to understand these kinds of things that had gone on, including him, of course. He was very, very generous in helping me. He said, at the outset, "You will find that I did a lot of things wrong. I got very angry with her a lot of the time. It's right on the tape. But you know, one of the things that the tapes were for was so she could say, 'You get things wrong, you know. Look at this. You're not supposed to act out, you're the doctor.' " He thought that this was very good for her—that it was very good for her to be able to have the memory, have the notes to come back to, and also to begin to, in fact, interact with him around it all by taking charge of it. So this great treasure came at great cost, because naturally it slowed me down to listen to them, but I also decided that I really had to rewrite the book. I couldn't use what I had written, because I now had a completely different set of sources, and I began putting those together into the story that I eventually told.

Listening to her interact with him gave me a sense of her presence so much. She was there very fully in her voice. I feel the range of things that you could hear in it that you could never read. When I tried to type it out—which I did; the book contains an appendix of a bit of the transcript of one of the tapes because I knew people would be curious about it—I had to invent a way to represent what was going on in that tape. Silence is terribly important; emphasis is very important. When I would transcribe everything and leave enough blank to say, "Now this much silence passes," it would become unreadable. It's not possible literally to transcribe a real interaction. You can't make any sense of it, so I had to invent a way to represent it. Again, it was like the portrait. It isn't the real thing. It's only a version of it, and this is the best I can do. Here it is.

The experience of the encounter with Anne Sexton,

and particularly listening to the both of them, was a real education for me. It gave me a confidence in understanding, [although] it wasn't really very useful in the sense of using a lot of [the taped material]. It let me know things, understand things, but I didn't quote a lot of it. Nonetheless, I feel that the book gains the confidence that I have that I really understand many of the complexities of the things that she was trying to do and understand in herself. I think I understood her treatment fairly well too. It's a really unique kind of archival resource that I hope eventually ends up at the University of Texas itself, so that in the future, after the death of everybody [mentioned] in the tape, other people can study this therapy.

WILMER: . . . I can't help but say something about your wish that the tapes of the therapy hour would end up in HRC [Harry Ransom Humanities Research Center at the University of Texas in Austin]. I hope they don't end up in HRC. I think that confidentiality transcends death. It is a questionable thing to give a patient's records to anybody, let alone put it in a depository, no matter how controlled it is, without the patient's written consent.

There are a lot of raunchy biographies that are published now. So a dark shadow is cast over the ethics of biography. But this is natural and only shows that the unethical behavior of some biographers or psychiatrists does not discredit biography or psychiatry. You can find a lot that's wrong with a person without being there at the time; you know, there is so much and you are aware of that. So I think that is a strange commentary on her psychiatrist. But, like any good reporter or biographer, you must use and will use what is given to you and be thankful for it. I'm talking as an analyst.

MIDDLEBROOK: I understand that. I'm sure that is going to be a big question. I hope that I get a chance to answer that. I'm sure I will, in fact, in a number of ways.

WILMER: I don't think there is an answer.

MIDDLEBROOK: Yes, there is.

WILMER: What is it?

MIDDLEBROOK: It's this. I understand the confidentiality issue. The doctor, Orne, said that yes, the confidentiality issue is very significant, but these tapes have a unique status in that they belong to the development of a poet who worked from them herself, who really used them in the development of herself as an artist and who was, in fact, proud of the achievement that she made. She herself had a sort of attitude that the tapes were a sort of unique developmental thing between her and him. They were not made in order to be in an archive. But they do uniquely belong to the development of a uniquely creative individual. He thought that the family's permission was sufficient to permit their use. And I agree. I think that there are certain kinds of project papers that belong to the rest of us after a time when the privacy of others is no longer at stake. I think that everybody who is mentioned in the tape should be dead before anybody else hears them. I have not mentioned the names or any material or information about living people without their permission that I gained from the tapes. So to have them sealed for a period of time until everybody's dead . . . These are a great human document, I believe. And I believe that the cultural property argument could be introduced here—that they belong to history, that they are uniquely valuable, that one of them in the world is enough, but that this one belongs to everybody and that a library that will protect the privacy of living individuals for a period of time so no one is hurt by their release would be the right place for them to go.

WILMER: Well, I obviously don't agree with you. It's one of the pitfalls of psychiatrists treating famous or "unique" people. I've seen that whenever you have a special person, that creates real transference and countertransference problems. So I don't believe in this unique person speciality. Jung and Freud both put down their psychological wisdom before the artists, the real artists. There is no way in which you can understand it. I think it can be argued as you have. I just don't agree with you.

The trust that Anne Sexton shared with her psychiatrist must surely be distorted by his use of the tapes. The relationship can hardly be called "close" when exposed to such a degree. This closeness would further degenerate if the tapes were turned over to the HRC. "Doctors have no obligation to history and certainly should not act as a research assistant to a biographer," Dr. Willard Gaylin, a Columbia University professor of psychiatry and an expert on medical ethics, commented in a *New York Times* article that set the pace for the exploration into the issue of Dr. Orne's behavior.[4] Dr. Gaylin described Dr. Orne's action as a betrayal of his patient and his profession.

There can be no betrayal unless there is first closeness and trust. There can be no closeness unless there is a belief that there will be no betrayal. The privacy of confessional or intimate relationships is possible only if the confessor expects that the confidences will not be broadcast. This was not the case of Dr. Orne in regard to Anne Sexton. He deemed Sexton's therapy public domain and believed that she would have wanted the tapes released, an opinion that Middlebrook agreed with.

In response to the *New York Times* article, Middlebrook wrote a letter to the editor in which she reinforced her belief that these tapes should "belong to everyone."

> . . . It seemed to us that the tapes provided a historical record of the processes by which a human being had survived a mental illness by turning her treatment into an education in the service of art.
>
> The tapes made me privy not only to anguish but also to thousands of homey particulars that make up an actual life. This was surely the rarest privilege ever conferred on a biographer. . . .[5]

Middlebrook, feeling that "this was surely the rarest privilege ever conferred on a biographer," reasoned that for the sake of history and cultural understanding she had no alternative but to transcend whatever medical or ethical concerns there might be. But to claim that "providing a historical record of the processes by which a human being had survived a mental illness by turning her treatment into an education in the service of art" is an opinion that would require extensive critical documentation by several competent psychiatrists and psychologists who had listened to all the audio tapes and read all the notes of the therapy.

Articles and letters in many newspapers and magazines followed the *New York Times* with sensational headlines such as "Trust Is at Stake," "Confidentiality Survives Death," and "Secrets of the Couch." The majority disapproved of Dr. Orne's actions and supported the precedent that popular interest should never be placed above confidentiality. In a *Newsweek* article Sexton's close friend Maxine Kumin scoffed at such opinions and claimed, "I feel it's self-serving for them to say Orne betrayed her. . . . The Sexton case is absolutely unique in the importance of her therapy to the development of her art. . . ."[6]

Everyone's life story is distinctive, and all therapy of creative people is unique. One of the problems in psychotherapy and analysis is trying not to treat creative people as different or make exceptions for them. The closeness that psychiatrists feel toward their "unique" patients must have strong boundaries. When the boundaries are crossed, psychiatrists are easily swept into the pull of their patient's fame and the person is lost along the way.

Dr. Orne, in his foreword to *Anne Sexton: A Biography*, writes:

> I also realized that Anne herself would have wanted to share this process—much as she did her poetry—so that other patients and therapists might learn from it. After much soul-searching, and after being assured that Anne's family had given their encouragement and approval, I allowed Professor Middlebrook to have access to the audiotapes and my therapy file. . . .[7]

No written evidence that Dr. Orne actually had the permission of Sexton's executor before he handed over the three hundred hours of audio tapes and his clinical records is presented. He knew that the family had consented to allow Middlebrook access to four tapes and other materials, but that was not the same as consenting to the release of his own professional notes and tapes. It is possible that since he is never explicit on this point, he only *assumed* they would grant consent based on their generous cooperation with Middlebrook and acquired their consent later, after the tapes were already turned over. Linda Gray Sexton, Anne Sexton's daughter and literary executor, admitted in a letter to the *New York Times* that she did not even know of the existence of the tapes before 1986, one year after he made his generous offer of the tapes to Middlebrook.[8]

While Dr. Orne sacrificed his closeness with Sexton for the sake of cultural property, her next psychiatrist sacrificed his intimacy with her for an even more dubious cause—his personal desire. Middlebrook discloses that after Dr. Orne moved to Philadelphia, Sexton had an affair with her next psychiatrist, whom the *Times* revealed to be Dr. Frederick Duhl but whom Middlebrook refers to pseudonymously as Dr. Ollie Zweizung. It is worth thinking about that name. The first name "Ollie" adds a flavor of intimate humor to the sardonic "Zweizung." The German adjective *"zweizüngig"* means "double-tongued" or "insincere."

There is no question that Sexton was betrayed with this intimacy. Effective therapy cannot take place when clouded by such involvement. Dr. Duhl disastrously compromised his healing powers as a psychiatrist when he established this relationship. While Sexton gained leverage over Dr. Duhl as his lover, she lost the chance to receive the objective guidance she needed so desperately.

Dr. Duhl treated the sexual encounters with Sexton as therapy and continued to charge her for the visits. Certainly she gained a new topic to explore in her poetry, but psychiatrists are not supposed to create perverse situations, but to examine and remedy existing ones.

Dr. Orne, aware of the affair, confronted both of them and reprimanded Dr. Duhl for his unconscionable behavior. But rather than expose Sexton to the trauma of losing her psychiatrist or Dr. Duhl to the risk of losing his license, he went no further.

While some people may gain from learning about the trauma in Sexton's life, there is a need for caution in looking at her story as a drama held behind closed doors. When a life is reduced to being viewed in such terms, it is easier to justify manipulating it. This was certainly the case with Sexton's psychiatric treatment. Her experiences of closeness and intimacy were ultimately used by others for purposes unrelated to her well-being.

NOTES

1. Diane Wood Middlebrook, *Anne Sexton: A Biography* (Boston: Houghton Mifflin Co., 1991).
2. Professor Middlebrook made a few editorial changes in the transcribed material to clarify her position for publication.
3. This included four audio tapes of her sessions with Dr. Orne that were found among her papers and placed at the Harry Ransom Humanities Research Center at the University of Texas at Austin, and do not include the three hundred audio tapes in Dr. Orne's possession.
4. *New York Times*, July 15, 1991, p. A1.
5. Letters to the Editor, *New York Times,* July 26, 1991.
6. *Newsweek*, July 29, 1991.
7. In Middlebrook, *Anne Sexton*, p. xvii.
8. *New York Times*, August 18, 1991.

An Approach to Closeness
Dream Sharing in a Small-Group Setting

Montague Ullman

This chapter highlights my experience with a small-group process designed to help a dreamer bridge the gap between dream image and waking reality. Dream sharing in such a setting relates to the theme of closeness in a number of ways. Dreamwork involves experimenting with a unique level of self-disclosure made possible by the support of the group and the nonintrusive way help is offered. This experience has a freeing effect. More of the self comes to the surface and is acknowledged. There are fewer impediments in the way of honest and close ties to others. Dream sharing generates a feeling of communion. There is also something intrinsic to dreaming which, when brought to life, can move us toward a more unified sense of ourselves as members of a single species. Asleep and dreaming, we seem able to focus on the disconnections in our lives, disconnections from our own past, and disconnections from others.

A few words about the nature of dreaming are in order.

Images that find their way into the dream are borrowed from waking life but are rearranged to form timely metaphorical reflections of the dreamer's subjective state at the moment. Metaphor is the distinctively human way of capturing glimpses of feelings not yet fully manifest. We use this talent at the onset of dreaming consciousness when we express the residual feelings that are left over from the day before in appropriate imagery. Further visual metaphorical representations evolve as these feelings reverberate through our memory system. What we end up with is a series of scenes metaphorically constructed and metaphorically interconnected. By the way they succeed in containing or releasing feelings, they serve as an internal signal. Either all is well and the dreaming phase of sleep continues to its natural end, or what has been stirred up is best dealt with through awakening. In sum, the dreamer explores the historically based ramifications of a current issue, mobilizes whatever resources are available, and attempts to contain the resulting feelings in the metaphorical imagery he or she has created.

Since we confront these issues in dreams using a primarily metaphorical language, we might begin by noticing the way writers or poets use metaphor. For them, metaphor serves as the vehicle for getting closer to the realities that are deeper than our ordinary discourse can denote. Take, for instance, a reference to the writings of Thoreau.

> Metaphor serves as his principal surveyor's tool, the "gauge" or "Realometer" by which he gains some leverage amid the mud and slush of opinion, and prejudice, and tradition and delusion. He is never more to the point than when speaking in figures; *here is where he pries the real apart from the language that encrusts it,* and in doing so gives things their real names: "The house is still but a sort of porch at the entrance of a burrow." [My italics][1]

Or consider the following view of metaphor as taking us beyond where we could go without it: "Beyond a certain level of evidence, system and knowledge fail and we fall back on metaphor, that recourse to living experience that apparently explains but, in fact, over time proves simply to complicate and thereby generate the need for further explanation."[2]

In dreamwork we seek to retrieve feelings embedded in images we ourselves have created. We trace them to their origins in recent and remote residues and, in doing so, liberate the feelings metaphorically represented.

We generate these night images spontaneously and involuntarily. We experience them as our immediate reality, not a symbolic one, and we respond as if we were captives of that reality. While asleep and dreaming, we respond to the images and not to their metaphorical meaning. They should more properly be referred to as potential metaphors. They can be appreciated as metaphors only when we waken and work out the two poles of the metaphor— the image and its connection to specific life experience. While we dream, we react to the feeling or lack of feeling associated with the imagery in the dream. That dreams may be available to us to explore further when we are awake is a gift from the night, incidental but none the less valuable.

DREAM SHARING IN A SMALL-GROUP SETTING

I have given a full description of the group process elsewhere.[3] In brief, it consists of structuring a small group to offer maximum help to the dreamer without being intrusive. Since it avoids the theoretical and technical strategies of formal therapy, its sole purpose is to help the dreamer appreciate, to the extent of his or her own readiness, all that the images can convey about the current emotional context of his or her life. Group members are oriented to meet the dreamer's two basic needs. The first is to feel safe. I refer to this as the Safety Factor. So that the dreamer may share the dream with others and engage in the self-disclosure necessary, an atmosphere of trust and safety must be created. This is brought about in a number of ways. The dreamer has complete control of the process. The dreamer determines the level of sharing and is free to stop the process at any point. No one in the group assumes the role of therapist. There is no imposition of any inter-pretive system. Trust is further generated by the way the group meets a second need of the dreamer—to discover what the dream is saying that would be difficult to discover alone. I refer to that as the Discovery Factor. Various strategies are used toward this end.

Briefly outlined, the process proceeds as follows:

Someone volunteers to share a dream and does so, giving as complete an account as possible of the dream as recalled and without going into associations or interpretive comments. It should be stressed that the decision to share a dream is the free choice of the dreamer. No one person is constrained to share a dream, regardless of the length of time they have been in the group. Whatever constraint does exist is the general constraint of being in a dream group to learn about dreams.

The second stage is an exercise or game in which each group member makes the dream his or her own. The members share with each other the feeling tones and moods the imagery evokes and then breathe metaphorical life into the dream by offering, from their own experience and imagination, ideas about how the imagery might connect with possible life experiences. They talk of the dream in the first person, address each other, not the dreamer, and all that they come up with is considered their own projection. By projecting feelings and thoughts onto the images, they are creating a reservoir of possibilities in the hope that some of them may have meaning for the dreamer. Often this happens. We all swim about in the same social sea and may very well use an image in the same way the dreamer did. The dreamer does not participate actively at this stage, but in the privacy of his or her psyche is free to accept or reject anything that comes from the group.

At the end of this stage, the dream is returned to the dreamer, who is then invited to respond. The dreamer is free to shape the response in any manner he or she chooses and to share at the most comfortable level of self-disclosure. At all times, the dreamer is responsible for setting the limits.

By this time, the dreamer has generally begun to move further into the dream. Should the dreamer wish to continue, a dialogue then ensues in which the members of the group question the dreamer to elicit as many associations as possible about the imagery of the dream. The questions are simply instruments for the dreamer to use to explore his or her psyche. The dreamer is free to go with the questions or not. The first set of questions is designed to help explore and reconstruct the emotional climate the dreamer experienced the night of the dream.

Again at the dreamer's invitation, two further strategies are applied. In the first, the dream is read back to the dreamer one scene at a time. The dreamer now has the initial information mustered when the dream was first returned plus additional information about the relevant current life context that group members brought out in the first phase of the dialogue. With greater contextual clarity, the dreamer is now able to build further bridges between the dream imagery and recent and remote emotional residues. The aim of playing the dream back in this way is to further contextualize the dream to the point where the dreamer becomes more and more aware of those aspects of the life experience and personality that the dream's evolving visual metaphors depict.

The final strategy is one in which members of the group are free to offer "orchestrating projections" to the dreamer. If anyone in the group sees a connection between dream image and the information the dreamer has shared, a connection not yet seen by the dreamer, he or she is free to offer it to the dreamer. It remains a projection unless validated by the dreamer.

The general aim is to help the dreamer bring out all the relevant information and so create the likelihood that connections will emerge spontaneously. The "orchestration" by the group is a strategy of last resort. Throughout, the group functions as a catalytic agent by trying to help the dreamer make explicit what is implicit in the imagery. The reality captured in the dream is brought into the waking mode through a social process that offers support and stimulation to the dreamer. This leads to significant and helpful readjustments in the dreamer's self-perception.

The notion of healing can be applied appropriately to dreamwork in a number of ways. These relate to the nature of dream content, the way in which dreamwork is carried out, the altered relationship of the dreamer to his or her own dreams as a consequence of dreamwork, and the changes that occur in relationship to others.

THE CONTENT OF DREAMS

All of us continually rework the emotional heritage of our past. Our dreams help us do this in rather remarkable ways. When some vulnerable area is exposed in the course of our daily life, the dream takes the initiative in tracking it down to its historical origins. Our dream seems to have access to deeper informational sources than are ordinarily available. Since we are always honest with ourselves while dreaming, the information we come up with is reliable. Jung spoke most movingly about this feature of our dream life when he wrote: "So flowerlike is it in its candor and veracity that it makes us blush for the deceitfulness of our lives."[4]

The dream's relevance to our current life situation, the historical prespective it affords, and the honesty of the self-scrutiny that ensues are the qualities of the imagery that make their explication a healing experience. The result of dreamwork is a movement toward greater clarity and openness, not about a trivial aspect of our life but around an issue from our past that has intruded into the present in a way that has set up an unresolved tension.

THE PROCESS OF DREAMWORK

Consciously or unconsciously, people tend to seek out emotionally healing experiences. One way these can occur is through dreams. There is something interesting about the curiosity everyone has about dreams. It is more than idle curiosity. I believe it hides a deeper awareness that dreams speak to hidden truths about our nature. With the dream comes an insistent urge to get at those truths. It is as if, at some level, we all recognize the validity of the Swedish author Poul Bjerre's characterization of the dream as a "natural healing system."[5] Quite early in the century, Bjerre took issue with Freud and saw dreams as a readily available route to healing. His writings demystified dreams and showed how the understanding of dreams could help everyone in everyday life. Jung, who was more intuitive and insightful about dreams than Freud, pursued the same path.

In contrast to physiological healing, emotional healing takes place outside the physically defined limits of the person. It happens because of changes that occur in an interpersonal field. Other people are an essential component of emotional healing. Emotional difficulties start with human beings and are resolved through human beings. Dreamwork evolves best in the context of an interpersonal field. The process I have described is so structured as to elicit and maximize the ability of others to function in a healing way toward the dreamer. This effects the release of the dreamer's own self-healing potential. Accompanied by, supported by, and stimulated by the group, the dreamer shares secrets, and a truer version of the self emerges.

In group dreamwork, general and specific factors contribute to the healing effect. The general factors include:

1. The rapid generation of trust in a nonintrusive atmosphere created by the structure.
2. The concern with and respect for the dreamer that are built into the process.
3. The sense of mutuality and commonality of experience that is generated by the way the group members, through their projections, share aspects of themselves with the dreamer.
4. The lack of a hierarchical structure. The leader assumes no special professional role and has the same option to share dreams as everyone else. His or her special responsibility is to lead the group thorugh the process. In all other respects, he or she functions as one of the group members. This flattening arrangement makes for greater sharing.

The specific factors involved arise in connection to the

way the group makes it easier for the dreamer to respond to the metaphors of the dream. The group's ability to open up the dream for the dreamer begins first with the range and virtuosity of the members' own projections and later is furthered by the skill and effectiveness with which they carry out the dialogue.

THE DREAMER AND THE DREAM

As dreamwork develops, the relationship of the dreamer to the dream changes. From being accidental, intrusive, strange, and sometimes frightening visitations, dreams are transformed into useful communications that contain information of value to the dreamer. Dreamwork becomes demystified. Participants sense the potential accessibility of the dream and obtain an awareness that when the dream is pursued in a supportive social context, the dreamer becomes better known to himself or herself and to others in a way that has elements of release and a sense of greater wholeness. The freedom to let oneself be known to others is also the freedom to be oneself.

One learns not to judge a dream on the basis of the immediate reactions it produces. These largely reflect the set and bias of the waking state. To judge a dream by the standards of the waking state (for example, whether it is deemed interesting or not) is also misleading and prejudicial. Such judgments are irrelevant to the nature of the dream. The dreamer soon learns that the only thing of importance is the connection the imagery has to a larger and more truthful version of the self. Regardless of the waking impression it produces, the dream comes to be looked upon as an available and helpful private resource.

THE DREAMER AND OTHERS

Healthy changes occur in the dreamer's own interpersonal milieu. The dreamer has been given privileged glimpses deep into the souls of other people and has seen there the same mix of vulnerability and strength that he or she has come to see in himself or herself. The dreamer has had the rare experience of witnessing people coming together as healers for each other. The dreamer has learned how to participate in healing others as well as himself or herself. There is a deepening appreciation of self and others and a growing sense of communion. The dreamer has greater awareness of the circumstances under which other people live, a greater sensitivity to the struggle that is part of being alive, and a greater interest in and tolerance for others. There is a healthier expansion and deepening of the social field and, as a result, a greater openness to new experience and competence in interpersonal relations.

Dreamers benefit not only from what the dream says, but also from how it is said. They come to recognize and appreciate, sometimes for the first time, the range of their own creativity and how it keeps them supplied with an unending source of useful imagery. When so motivated, dreamers can channel this creative source into artistic and aesthetic outlets in the waking state. They experience nighttime imagery as a hidden creative resource that is there for their benefit and can be called upon when needed.

Many of my views on the nature of the dream have changed with my growing experience with group dreamwork, an experience that included not only training psychotherapists but also efforts to extend dreamwork into the community. The changes I refer to involve the technique and nature of dreamwork. Broader issues have arisen with implications that go beyond dreamwork and relate to all other modalities where imagery is used to shed light on unconscious processes.

CHANGES RELATED TO DREAMWORK ITSELF

It is a truism that a dreamer generally needs help to fully realize the meaning embedded in the imagery. Ever since Freud defined dreamwork as the province of someone psychoanalytically trained, the role of the helper has been considered to be a professional one. I regard this as unnecessarily constraining. The role of the helper does not have to be defined professionally, and serious dreamwork can be carried on outside the framework of a formal therapeutic engagement. The skills necessary for dreamwork can be taught. They involve learning how the visual metaphor expresses meaning symbolically and learning how to help a dreamer elaborate on the recent and remote feeling residues that shaped the dream. The skills also involve learning how to listen to all that the dreamer says in an open, unbiased way and how to ask questions that can be helpful in elucidating the relevant life context without going beyond whatever limits the dreamer sets.

Perhaps the most significant change from a technical point of view involves the way I see the operation of defense mechanisms. I no longer view them as quite as difficult to influence as I did during my career as a psychoanalyst. I see them as much more responsive to the social milieu and much more apt to melt away in an atmosphere of safety and trust. Put another way, in the presence of a supportive and stimulating social milieu, the dreamer's own curiosity will override his or her defensiveness.

Group work with dreams has made me more aware of some of the limitations of one-on-one dreamwork in formal therapy. These include time limitations since the patient may have many more items than the dream on the agenda; the limitations imposed by the nature of the hierarchical arrangement where dream sharing goes only one way and someone else other than the dreamer is looked up to as the expert; and the temptation, at least with inexperienced therapists, to misuse theory in a way that aborts the search for information. The therapist has the advantage, or course, of knowing the dreamer in greater depth. This can be a two-edged sword since the therapist may respond along a too narrow path based on past experience with the patient, and the response can result in an insufficient tracking of what is happening now.

Psychoanalytically, I was not brought up as a Jungian, but the group dreamwork I have done has brought me closer to Jung's notion of an underground psychic terrain common to all of us. As members of a single species, we have a common underlying psychic dimension to our existence that unites us in our struggle for survival as a species. The hallmark of this heritage is a sensitivity to what is true despite the frantic efforts at times of our higher faculties to obliterate the truth.

We all have certain basic needs, and this "universal unconscious" of ours does its best to see that those needs are met regardless of how astray we go in the pursuit of personal goals. Living organisms have to be in touch with what is real. Our complex symbolic superstructures some-times cause difficulties, obscuring rather than highlighting the real. In the group situation, when we work with someone else's dream, we clear the way for the maximum display of our connectedness to what is real. This is a somewhat different view of Jung's concept of the collective unconscious. But I think it embodies his emphasis on the universality of this dimension of our existence, its ability to counter the one-sidedness of waking life and in gyroscopic fashion enable us to remain upright in the face of ever-increasing social forces threatening to upset our balance, and finally, in his notion of archetypes, sensing that a bridging mechanism exists between our tissue needs and the symbolic superstructures we have erected.

What follows, admittedly speculative, are some of the broader issues that arise from our remarkable capacity to generate spontaneously meaningful imagery.

Dreaming and Connectedness
This first issue concerns the dreamer's affective connection to others. While dreaming, we confront ourselves with the state of our connections to significant others in our lives, the strategies we use to undermine or restore these connections, and the social pressures that place obstacles in our paths. The essence of the dream's natural healing potential derives from the dreamer's ability to produce imagery that reflects recently exposed areas of *disconnection* to others or to oneself. By this I mean that the dreamer is concerned with ongoing events or experiences that significantly affect the felt sense of connectedness to others. Such experiences set off reverberating tremors at different levels and define the issue to be explored in the dream.

The relationship of dreams to connectedness emerges clearly in the course of group dreamwork. In the presence of a safe atmosphere generated by the nonintrusive nature of the process, social defenses melt away or, at any rate, do not interfere with the deep-level sharing and sense of communion that are generated. Group members are able to respond at a feeling level to someone else's imagery. We can partially understand this in terms of a shared social milieu. The response may also be due to the deeper way imagery has of linking people together that is more akin to a shared aesthetic response.

Dreaming and the Survival of the Species

The dream's ability to reflect the dreamer's concern with maintaining connections has led me to speculate that while asleep and dreaming, we are engaged with a much deeper aspect of our human nature than when we are awake, an aspect that goes beyond the concerns of the individual. Group dreamwork discloses an agency that works against fragmentation. Trust, and a sense of solidarity, develop rapidly in a dream-sharing group. I suggest that the concern wth connectedness links dreaming to a larger issue, namely the survival of the species.

The evolution of the human species has been characterized not only by diversity but also by a remarkable degree of disunity. Separations and tensions have arisen in many different ways. We have drawn lines between ourselves and others according to country of origin, color of skin, religious preference, class position, and so on. At some level, each of us is a victim of the emotional fallout from this continuing process. In this nuclear age, who among us does not harbor some concern about whether we will establish collaborative ties among nations that are strong enough to avert a nuclear catastrophe? Each of us plays a role in mitigating or perpetuating this now dangerous situation.

It is as if while dreaming we display where we are in relation to this state of affairs from our personal and immediate point of veiw. Somewhere within us is an awareness that, if unchecked, this disunity could be the seed for our eventual destruction. Only through constructive, affective bonding can this fragmentation be overcome and the species endure.

While dreaming, we seem able to transcend individual boundaries and move toward our place in a larger whole. The images we create register alienating pressures intrinsic to our social environment and the way we have come to deal with such pressures in our day-to-day encounter with others. It is in this sense that dreams may be perceived as arising from a built-in mechanism concerned with the survival of the species. The individual's effort to maintain a sense of connectedness is part of the larger concern, namely, the issue of species connectedness. Poets, writers, and, in their own way, psychotics, have always seemed to know about this connectedness and to relate to it. Creative artists express it in a way that can be appreciated by others. Psychotics manipulate it to fit in with their autistic vision.

To support the idea that we view our underlying connectedness from two entirely different perspectives, those of waking and sleeping, I will bring together an unlikely pair, an odd couple. Despite their disparate origins, interests, and ways of life, each has something important to say about this question of interconnectedness.

The first member of the pair is August Strindberg, that fascinating, complex, and unhappy genius. Harry G. Carlson, in his study of Strindberg's use of mythical themes in his plays, notes Strindberg's preoccupation with the Indian concept of *maya*, a term that refers to "the tissue of objects, things, and people that constitute what men believe to be reality. . . ."[6] He traces Strindberg's interest to his reading of Schopenhauer:

> It is difficult to pinpoint exactly when Strindberg became familiar with maya or maya-like concept, but it might have been as early as the 1870s, the time he first became impressed by Schopenhauer. Maya is a basic and recurrent expression in *The World as Will*, where we

find scores of passages like the following: "The eyes of the uncultured individual are clouded, as the Indians say, by the veil of maya. To him is revealed not the thing-in-itself, but only the phenomenon in time and space. . . . In this form of his limited knowledge he sees not the inner nature of things, which is one, but its phenomena *as separated, detached, innumerable, very different, indeed opposed.*" Part of Agnes' mission in *A Dream Play* is to help mortals understand that they see not "the inner nature of things, which is one," but the multiplicity, the misleading, illusory veil of maya, "phenomena as separated, detached, innumerable, very different, indeed opposed." [My italics][7]

Strindberg's writings reveal his own desperate struggle to resolve his deep feelings of disconnection with the social order of his day (he exiled himself from Sweden during a critical part of his life), and his almost pitiful struggle to make a go of married life and fatherhood. The fires of absolute individualism consumed him to the point of psychotic-like behavior at times. He ended up bypassed socially (the Nobel committee chose another Swede, one generally considered a lesser writer) and alienated from friends and family.

The second member of this pair, David Bohm, a distinguished theoretical physicist, postulates an underlying order of reality not directly knowable, but constituting the ground of all being. He refers to this as the Implicate Order. Out of this, an Explicate Order arises. In Bohm's words:

The essential feature of this idea was that the whole of the universe is in some way enfolded in everything and that each thing is enfolded in the whole. From this it follows that in some ways, and to a certain degree, everything enfolds or implicates everything. The basic proposal is that this enfoldment relationship is not merely passive or superficial. Rather, it is active and essential to what each *is*. It follows that each thing is internally related to the whole and, therefore, to everything else. The external relationships are then displayed in the unfolded or *explicate* order in which each thing is seen as separate and extended and related only externally to other things. The explicate order, which dominates ordinary experience as well as classical physics, is secondary, however, in the sense that ultimately it flows out of the primary reality of the implicate order.

Because the implicate order is basically dynamic in nature, I called it holomovement. All things found in the unfolded explicate order emerge from the holomovement in which they are enfolded as potentialities, and ultimately they fall back into it. They endure only for a time, and while they last, their existence is sustained in a constant process of enfoldment and reenfoldment, which gives rise to the relatively stable and independent forms in which they appear in the explicate order.[8]

We are part of the explicate order, but we can never see the whole of it, only what our perceptual apparatus allows us to see. Through the way we perceive this explicate order, we create a perceptual order, which Alex Comfort refers to as consensus reality or middle-order reality. In his discussion of Bohm, Comfort puts it this way:

We have accordingly a threefold structure, an underlying extra-dimensional field or pattern, a manifest order generated from it by the process he terms explication, and ordinary middle-order reality generated from the manifest world by our perception of it.[9]

Comfort is using the term "manifest order" to encompass the entire explicate order whereas our waking grasp of that order is limited to how we have learned to perceive it. As a result of long conditioning, our perceptual order takes discreteness as the primary given despite our ever deepening understanding of field interrelationships. Bohm suggests, and I think rightly so, that this approach to understanding the nature of reality has played an important role in fostering the degree of alienation and fragmentation that now exists in the world today.

What unifies Strindberg's interest in *maya* and Bohm's explicate order is that in both instances we are said to settle for a limited, fragmented, and one-sided view of reality and to lose sight of the deeper structure of interconnectedness that pervades this order. We fail to appreciate the profound significance of what Bohm refers to as the "unbroken wholeness" that characterizes all of nature.

How do the considerations offered about dreaming tie in with the constructs emphasized by Bohm? In a general and analogous way, the view presented here is more intrinsically related to notions of interconnectedness and "unbroken wholeness" than are dream theories designating reified psychic entities at war with each other. Awake, we are mired in our own discreteness and, by the language we use, trapped by the seeming discreteness of all else about us. Asleep and dreaming, we forsake linguistic categories as a primary mode of expression. We risk feeling our way back into this underlying unity and set ourselves the task of exploring both internal and external hindrances to the full range of the manifest order and its rootedness in a deeper order of connectedness. Bohm's notion of "unbroken wholeness," which characterizes the implicate order, is like an insistent Greek chorus, heard dimly or not attended to at all during our waking hours. Awake and tied to the perceptual order, we tend to see things in their discreteness. Waking consciousness is narrowly focused on the immediate reality facing us. We experience this against a background of feeling tones, emotional murmurings derived from our historical background. While dreaming, we affect a figure-ground reversal, one that brings aspects of that "unbroken wholeness" more into focus.

In Bohm's terms, we might say that metaphor is the instrument that carries us deeper into the interplay of these two orders once some newly revealed aspect of that interplay begins to affect our life. Through metaphor, we reach out to what is still implicit, that which is unidentified, unconceptualized, and still only a dimly felt stirring within us. Its initial grasp defies the ordinary use of language, which is simply not up to the task. That language is of use only after metaphor has forced what has been implict out of its hiding place.

From this, it is easy to see how metaphor acts as a force propelling us into the future. It represents movement, change, a tampering with the unknown, an exploration of a mystery. Directed at the outside world through poetry, art, and even science, it brings more into the domain of the known. Directed to the inner world, it eases the passage of material from the domain of the unconscious to that of the conscious. In both instances, it offers to the creator of the metaphor and to those who benefit from its creation a more compelling connection to what is real.

The healing potential of dream imagery has been explored as a consequence of the experience I have had with dream groups. By calling attention to certain common attributes of dreaming and waking consciousness, I have suggested elsewhere[10] that the basic features of dreaming consciousness, namely, to display more of ourselves more honestly to ourselves, can be understood as phylogenetically derived manifestations of vigilance operations during the repetitive cycles of arousal that characterize mammalian sleep. Based on these considerations, along with the impact of group dreamwork, I have further suggested that the organizing principle underlying the adaptive significance of dreaming derives from operations relating to species survival.

Healing has been linked to our remarkable capacity while dreaming to produce an endless supply of meaningful metaphorical imagery. Eschewing any metapsychological considerations, I have felt the need to link dreaming consciousness to something else, not another metapsychological system, but to a different way of perceiving both inner and outer reality.

This brought me to Bohm's ideas about the implicate and explicate order. His conceptual scheme seemed to offer a way of appreciating the limitations of our perceptual apparatus in its dealings with the manifest or explicate order or reality and the consequent difficulties we encounter in an effort to delve more deeply into what still remains implicate within ourselves and in the world about us. Disengagement from the waking mode makes it possible for us to contact manifest reality in a way more congruent with the nature of that order than our waking perception of it. This is the goal we seek when we engage in dreamwork. The therapeutic value of the image lies in the use we can put it to while awake. By tapping into the information it contains, we move toward greater wholeness and greater freedom. In a term borrowed from physics, we experience a greater degree of "coherence" with the natural order of the world about and within us.

NOTES

1. Geoffrey O'Brien, "Thoreau's Book of Life," *New York Review of Books,* Jan. 15, 1987, p. 49.

2. Leigh Hafrey, "Write About What You Know: Big Bang or Grecian Urn," *New York Times Book Review*, Dec. 28, 1986, p. 8.

3. Montague Ullman and Nan Zimmerman, *Working with Dreams* (Los Angeles: Jeremy P. Tarcher, 1979); Montague Ullman and Claire Limmer, *The Variety of Dream Experience* (New York: Continuum, 1988).

4. C. G. Jung, *Psychological Reflections: An Anthology of the Writing of C. G. Jung,* selected and edited by Jolande Jacobi (New York: Pantheon Books, 1953), p. 46.

5. Poul Bjerre, *Drömmarnas Helande Kraft* (Stockholm: Proprius Förlag, 1982).

6. Harry G. Carlson, *Strindberg and the Poetry of Myth* (Berkeley, Calif.: University of California Press, 1982), p. 141.

7. Ibid., pp. 141–142.

8. David Bohm, "A New Theory of Mind and Matter," *Journal of the American Society for Psychical Research* 80, no. 2 (1986): 113–135.

9. Alex Comfort, "The Implications of an Implicate," *Journal of Social Biological Structure* 4 (1981): 363–374.

10. Montague Ullman, "Dreaming, Altered States of Consciousness and the Problem of Vigilance," *Journal of Nervous and Mental Disease* 133, no. 6 (1961): 529–535.

Transference/Countertransference

A Poem by Harry A. Wilmer

The manifestations of transference and countertransference as they relate to ethics, intimacy, distance, closeness, sex, and seduction are of immense practical importance from the perspective of those who are helping and those who are seeking help.

There are inevitable temptations, transgressions, and shameful abuses of this relationship. The temptations and fantasies of intimacy of *both* doctor and patient, supervisor and candidate, teacher and student are ubiquitous. The projections of love or hate between the two people are well known. Properly analyzed they are essential building blocks in the process of growth, understanding, and individuation. Without such projections the human elements of improvement and cure could not take place.

The following comments are excerpted from my book *Practical Jung: Nuts and Bolts of Jungian Psychotherapy* (Wilmette, Ill.: Chiron Publications, 1987).

Every therapist experiences love in the transference;
it's a kind of inevitable *rondo unconscioso* that is
projected by the patient onto the therapist.
We don't know how it happens or why it really
   happens,

therefore it is irrational.
What lies deeply buried in the psyche beyond
conscious comprehension is experienced outside in
    someone else.
There is always a reality basis,
some hook on which to hang the projection,
something that is actually loveable or hateable.
Hate in the transference is the same phenomenon.

The problem comes when the therapist takes it too
    personally.
The patient has to cope with something on top of
    the transference—
the countertransference.
The patient evokes love or hate in the therapist.
The big problem comes when the therapist is
    unconscious
of countertransference.

Sound complicated?
It is. But it is a key to human relationships.

Both transference and countertransference
have their roots in childhood,
in the repressed memories, feelings, and images
    from
parental figures or others who were very close
to the child.
These powerful feelings also have their source
in the actual relationship of patient and therapist.
It is important always to remember that the
    unconscious is unconscious until we become
    conscious of it;
even then it only comes to us in glimpses.

There are transferences and countertransference
    feelings
that do not come from our repressed personal life
    memories

but from the collective unconscious,
the deepest realm of the unconscious which is
our inherited psyche.
Every therapist encounters transference.
Every therapist experiences countertransference,
irrational thoughts and feelings about the patient,
    but
not all face transference and countertransference.
Many about-face to save face.

Countertransference implies that the therapist's
    transference
is evoked by the patient's transference.
That is not always the case.
It can be there on its own,
just like the patient's transference.

Often in subtle or not so subtle ways, the therapist
is caught in the web of transference-
    countertransference.
In every case it is the therapist's responsibility
not to be blind,
and to create a safe, caring space
in which the patient can face these projections,
and come to understand them without the danger
of being either victim or the victimizer
of strong unconscious forces.

The therapist is more than a blank screen,
more than an anonymous figure.
The therapist is real enough
and no more than enough.

The therapist also gets shadow projections
of badness, evil, hatred, jealousy, rage, and anger,
and of Olympian, omnipotent, godlike, and priestly
    powers.
Savior and guru: oh, it's so tempting to believe.

In the love-hate diathesis, the patient and therapist
are carried by powerful forces
between Charybdis and Scylla.

On Loving

A patient's erotic transference coupled
with a therapist's erotic countertransference
is a lusty, potent aphrodisiac.
For the therapist to take advantage of this
is to embezzle love.
You might call it incest.

Falling in love is both natural and magical.
Unfortunately, falling in love is also being mad.
It is not by chance that we speak of
falling under the spell of love.
Falling out of love is another matter.
But there are other ways of falling out.

RULE OF THUMB: Love Nitty Gritty
What do you say when a patient says:
    "I love you."
    "I dreamed I was sleeping with you."
    "What would you say if I told you I love you?"
    "Why do you blush? I know! You love me."
    "Why are you hiding your desire behind jargon?"
    "Can we meet for dinner or drinks?"
    "Let's get together and talk outside your office.
     OK?"

Not so fast. One at a time.

What do you say when a patient says, "I love you"?
You do not say, "What kind of stupid question are
   you asking me?"
Do you have cookbook answers up your sleeve?

Answers come in many languages and in countless
    volumes;
answers come from art, music, drama, and stories
and from prehistoric times.

Try again.
What do you say when a patient says, "I love you"?
I say yes in my own idiom, which means
message received, message accepted as your truth.
These feelings of love are feelings that naturally
    evolve in such
a relationship as this. The message is honored and
received empathetically.
You can remind yourself that
overt sexual behavior between therapist and patient
butchers psychotherapy.
Above all, after getting the message straight,
don't intellectualize!
That's a cop-out for either of you.

RULE OF THUMB: Sex
No.

Some psychotherapists have said that
there is nothing wrong with having sex with
    patients.
Would you believe it? You would? Oh!
Who's to blame for the consequences?
What? You don't assign blame if you're a
    psychotherapist? Ha!
Slick trick. That is prestidigitation.

The ultimate pay-off for the nonblaming therapist
is the mystique of nonblaming oneself.
We are all children of sham.
That is the painful truth.
It is our unending labor to rise above sham.

RULE OF THUMB: Using a Couch in Therapy
I gave my psychoanalytic couch away twenty years ago.
Some therapists like to use the couch.
It fosters regression which might be useful.
It might even be used by some therapists
to avoid a human relationship.
It matters that you remain conscious
of your sexual and power fantasies.

For some the couch is an icon.
For some it is handy, and for others, dandy
because it takes the patient out of eye contact.
Personally that is not a problem for me.
If it were, I would use the couch
because the fewer problems I have,
the more we can deal with the problems
that the patient has.

Suppose a patient says to you:
"What would you say if someone said they love
     you?"

Play it again, Sam. It's a sensitive subtle question.
Almost any question that any patient may ask can be
     managed by
reflecting on it seriously and in plain English.
If someone asked me:
"What would you say if someone said they love
     you?"
That person wants me to say,
"I love you."

Sex again? Sex with a patient?
Sex with a patient is not possible.
Sex is not possible with a patient, because
sex always transforms a relationship into something
     else.
Sex is not therapy.

It is the end of therapy.
Sex in psychotherapy is exploitative and destructive.
Sex with a patient?
Not a patient and therapist but an *it* and an *it*.

No doubt therapists and patients fall in love,
and once in a while they get married.
That is unfortunate but not necessarily
the end of anything but the therapy.

When there is love in the transference
that is the time, above all, to be empathic,
to retain your distance, your cool, and your
    equanimity.
Your aplomb too, if you think you might lose it.
That is the time for reason to prevail over feeling.
If managed properly nothing is lost and much is
    gained, and
psychotherapy becomes more interesting
and ever more likely to help.
But if mismanaged the therapy is shipwrecked.

RULE OF THUMB: Taking
You don't have to take everything that is offered.
As a matter of fact, you had better not.
The touchy-feely area of psychotherapy was a passing
    phase.

RULE OF THUMB: Sticky Fingers
Always keep your sticky fingers off sticky situations.

Falling in Love

Love develops naturally
in the intimate relationship of psychotherapy.
The love may range from caring to passion.
It is a model which helps us to understand love in the
    world.
Falling in love is the unreal idealization of the other,

a marvelous enchantment, a spellbinding fascination
with the image of the other.
Falling in love is conceptualized as a reciprocal
 anima-animus projection.
It is this which draws people into relationship
by creating a fantasy relatedness.
The inner image carried by the psyche is
projected onto a real other person and never quite
 fits.
But it is a good approximation.
As time goes on the glorious idealization
begins to be seen in the light of the real other
 person;
the projections are withdrawn.
Some people pretend this doesn't happen,
and a sham love relationship results,
but for others the withdrawal of projections
is the beginning of a real relationship—
affinity instead of infatuation,
deep caring instead of blind adoration.
This is the beginning of individuation and growth
in the relationship.
It is the same thing as psychotherapy.

RULE OF THUMB: What to Say
You can say almost anything to a patient
if you are not caught in countertransference love or
 hate.
If you are not covertly hostile or seductive
you will be astonished at the direct, candid,
and sham-free things you can say.
There is no more significant Rule of Thumb.

Eros always wounds but in wounding heals.
Yes, I do love my patient, but in a different way.
No, I do not love my patient, but I care and try to
 understand.

If I neither care nor love and am only in there
pitching, I might as well become a stockbroker.
In the end there is nothing extraordinary about
    therapy.
When the pupil is ready the teacher will appear.

Once a loving child said to me,
"You're not an ordinary M.D. You're a D.U."
Thinking, duodenal ulcer, I asked "What is a D.U.?"
"Oh, don't you know? That's Doctor of
    Understanding.
Like my best teacher."

A middle-aged man was telling me of a hassle
over making his adolescent son's lunch.
I asked him why he didn't let his son make his own
    lunch.
He turned on me with condescending hostility:
"And when did you start making your own lunch?"
"Not soon enough." The words had instantly come
    to me
as if from someone else.
There was a momentary double take,
then a smile crept over his face,
"I get it," he said.

Therapists wear an invisible toga
when they put on their helping persona.
This toga is preferable to putting on the dog,
but the hidden message symbolized
by the healing toga is that
we will not fail our patients,
we will not desert them, and
we will stay near them.
We will do our best to help them
because in the end, we will both have grown
and both become healthier.
We will have tolerated the kind of healthy hostility

that is lauded in the rotunda of the Jefferson
   Memorial
in Washington, D.C.:
I have sworn upon the altar of God
eternal hostility against every form of tyranny
over the mind of man.

Part Two

FAMILY
AND SOCIETY

A Social Attitude

Joseph L. Henderson

In recent years, I have been interested in trying to describe what I call the cultural attitudes to be found in any cultivated society. I consider that four basic cultural attitudes may exist separately or in tandem with others. In my book *Cultural Attitudes in Psychological Perspective*, I presented them in a certain order beginning with a "Social Attitude," followed by chapters on a "Religious Attitude," an "Aesthetic Attitude," and finally a "Philosophic Attitude."[1] The book ended with a section describing a "Psychological Attitude" that I felt was an outgrowth in modern times of the philosophic attitude. Altogether I developed hypotheses for four attitudes, and possibly a fifth: social, religious, aesthetic, philosophic, and psychological.

I drew my conclusions concerning these attitudes from observing many people, including acquaintances and friends. Above all, I observed my patients, with whom I was able to explore the validity of these attitudes in much greater depth than I could by simply observing their personalities and behavior. Occasionally I was also able to find evidence for my views accidentally in biographical accounts of the inner experiences of well-known figures in contemporary life. Golda Meir beautifully describes a social attitude in her autobiography; Alfred North Whitehcad reveals a philosophic attitude in his account of his life experience; Kenneth Clark shows a classic example of an aesthetic attitude in his autobiography.[2]

Sometimes I encountered a surprising reversal of my initial view of a person's cultural identity. An example of this occurred when I discovered the difference between two men's exposure to their basic cultural attitude while under the influence of psychedelic drugs. In *Zen Effects*, a biography of Alan Watts, I was struck with Aldous Huxley's description of his experience after taking four-tenths of a gram of mescaline:

> A flower vase on the table containing a rose, a carnation, and an iris, which had interested him briefly at breakfast, became the focus of his attention. "I was not looking now at an unusual flower arrangement. I was seeing what Adam had seen on the morning of his creation—the miracle, moment by moment, of naked existence.
>
> "Is it agreeable?" somebody asked.
>
> "Neither agreeable nor disagreeable," I answered. "It just is."
>
> The "Is-ness" (Istigkeit) of which Meister Eckhart had spoken—the Being of Plato—suddenly Huxley saw it in the flowers. "A transience that was yet eternal life, a perpetual perishing that was at the same time pure Being, a bundle of minute, unique particulars in which, by some unspeakable and yet self-evident paradox, was to be seen the divine source of all existence."[3]

In contrast to this is Alan Watts's description of his own drug-induced experience late one night in the garden of his house. He writes:

> The garden was a lawn surrounded by shrubs and high trees—pine and eucalyptus—and floodlit from the house

which enclosed it on one side. As I stood on the lawn I noticed that the rough patches where the grass was thin or mottled with weeds no longer seemed to be blemishes. Scattered at random as they were, they appeared to constitute an ordered design, giving the whole area the texture of velvet damask, the rough patches being the parts where the pile of the velvet is cut. In sheer delight I began to dance on this enchanted carpet, and through the thin soles of my moccasins I could feel the ground becoming alive under my feet, connecting me with the earth and the trees and the sky in such a way that I seemed to become one body with my whole surroundings.

Looking up, I saw that the stars were colored with the same reds, greens and blues that one sees in iridescent glass, and passing across them was the single light of a jet plane taking forever to streak over the sky. At the same time, the trees, shrubs, and flowers seemed to be living jewelry, inwardly luminous like intricate structures of jade, alabaster, or coral, and yet breathing and flowering with the same life that was in me. Every plant became a kind of musical utterance, a play of variations on a theme repeated from the main branches, through the stalks and twigs, to the leaves, the veins in the leaves, and to the fine capillary network between the veins. Each new bursting of growth from a center repeated or amplified the basic design with increasing complexity and delight, finally exulting in a flower.[4]

One might suppose that Aldous Huxley would exhibit an aesthetic attitude in his LSD fantasy since he was a creative writer, primarily a novelist. Instead we can see quite clearly that all his reactions speak of a religious attitude and perhaps a philosophic one. In contrast, Alan Watts was devoted to religious ideas and practices from an early age; Church of England religion and Zen Buddhist studies motivated his major work. Yet we find in Watts's account of his psychedelic experience a purely aesthetic reaction. All of this convinces me that Huxley had a religious attitude as a basic motivation for his work, and that Watts had an aesthetic attitude that was more deeply characteristic for him than his supposed religious attitude.

Those examples illustrate a fact that true cultural attitudes are not derived purely from educational influences but from a deep level of cultural conditioning, which is particularly true of the philosophic attitude. This attitude is conditioned by such age-old patterns of myth as the creation myths of primitive peoples, and by the more modern but deeply historical memory of number symbolism, as exemplified by the Pythagorean tetraktys or the Chinese H-t'u and Mo-Tu number series as Dr. Marie-Louise von Franz has shown in her book *Number and Time*.[5]

Does the social attitude also have a deep cultural root that exists subliminally so that it functions effectively only if there is a sufficiently strong need to contact and be nourished from this primordial? If so, this would help to validate not only the existence of such a social attitude but also confirm that deeper meaning underlying the other cultural attitudes as well.

I am going to begin on a personal, reminiscent level different from my formal presentation of this subject in my book. I was born in a small American town and lived there during my boyhood and early adolescence in the first part of this century. When, many years later, I read Sinclair Lewis's novel *Main Street*, I knew at once I had been diagnosed as having a specific cultural illness, a condition whereby provincialism breeds kindness, forbearance, and tolerance at the same time as it fosters suspicion, defensiveness, and conventionality of a particularly corrosive nature. In the worlds I later came to know,

I found, of course, the same pairs of opposites, but I also found a willingness to confront them and to some extent resolve their tension, rendering them more flexible to change. But in the cities, something of the country town had been lost, something preciously human and vulnerable that acknowledges the truth of social life, that honors both the bad and the good as part of the texture of daily life not subject to change. And this is what I have, in time, come to recognize as necessary for a true social attitude to be formed.

I have found this element in certain individuals and in certain social groups, and it is always the same—a social contract in the sense Rousseau described it, but more personal. I think of Thornton Wilder's play *Our Town* as a perfect example of this kind of community that is unchanging not because it is provincial but because human beings are in the long run part of something universal.

Without an emphasis on individual differences, there can be no effective social attitude so that we arrive at the paradox that the most truly individual is also the most truly social. I found this on a large scale during the eight years I lived in England in my twenties and early thirties. I used to be shocked at the deeply critical statements English people often made of each other in quite ordinary conversations. But I noticed that it did not seem to disturb or interrupt their interpersonal relationship. Living on an island for centuries has bred in them a sense of community but also a fear that if they come too close to each other without criticism they will fall into hatred if not paranoia. So they maintain this psychosocial balance between *closeness* and its necessary opposite, *separation*, for the sake of individual freedom.

In America, we have some of the same patterns of social relationship I have just described, and they have existed in many other countries as well. We could still learn from the English a particular kind of social exchange that is the basis of good government. In my book, I used the image of Hobbes's *Leviathan* as a cultural symbol for this kind of governing principle.[6] The frontispiece of this book, written in the seventeenth century, is of the enormous figure of man towering above the hills of a country landscape dotted with many villages, hamlets, and castles. A large, walled town occupies the foreground with its church prominent in the center. The human figure is composed of many, many small human figures packed close together. The subtitle informs us that this *Leviathan* means *The Matter, Form, and Power of a Commonwealth Ecclesiastical and Civil.* So it is the authority invested not in one man (this one bearing on his head a kingly crown and in one hand holding a scepter while in the other a sword), but in the social community that constitutes the body of this figure. He is both individual (that is a unity) and collective (that is a multiplicity).

I suggest that anyone with a true social attitude feels that he or she is part of a cultural organism consisting of many parts that, however, offer the widest capacity for feeling individuated on a social level. In other words, when social values embrace both individual and cultural needs, we have a condition that is ripe for attaining individuation in a social context. Marie-Louise von Franz expresses this well:

> In practical terms this means that the existence of human beings will never be satisfactorily explained in terms of isolated instincts, such as hunger, power, sex, survival, perpetuation of the species and so on. That is, man's purpose is not to eat, drink, etc., but to *be human* . . . , and for its expression the unconscious often chooses the powerful image of the *Cosmic Man.*[7]

People with a developed social attitude are humanitarian in the best sense of the word, and this "Leviathan" is the basic image of the society from which we all have emerged until recently. However, in our century, increasingly and alarmingly, we experience a deep discontent with our leaders where ecumenical religions function autonomously, and transitory heads of government control military forces. Jung frequently pointed out the psychological danger that the state per se may become a collective monster when we lose that sense of kingship that Hobbes's Leviathan embodied.

On the personal level, such a sense of kingship means self-control beyond the ego's fluctuating desires for power or pleasure. On a cultural level, it is, as we have said, a sense of belonging to a self-regulating community, a condition of balance that Victor Turner has called *societas* combining or integrating communal feeling with a structure to ensure its permanence. When one or both of these controlling energies fail, a sense of demoralization emerges, and an abyss opens to engulf individual human beings and the culture to which they belong. It may then happen that a deeper archetypal image appears that fully meets the requirement of von Franz's Cosmic Man. This is known from ancient times as an image called the Anthropos.

Jung has fully researched this image of the Anthropos throughout religious history in the Western world. The image goes all the way back to Egypt where it emerges from a primordial level of the unconscious as an animal, the baboon, known as Thoth, "visibly preserved all through the numberless editions of the *Book of the Dead* right down to recent times." It emerges into human forms as Hermes in Greece, and as Christ as Son of Man in the Christian period. These figures are still connected with archetypal roots spreading out into many areas, but chiefly they embrace or embody the four elements: air, earth, fire, and water. They also "are associated with roundness and also squareness." In another version, the Anthropos is hermaphroditic as a combination of the opposites in a religious sense. But this religious tradition is not merely religious; it contains the whole nature of man that expresses his social identity in the world. We therefore can evoke this sense of the *all* and the *one* in the famous quote from Terrence's play: "I am a man and nothing human is alien to me. . . ." "Human" here means cultivated, Gerhard Dorn's *vir unis*, or true man, of which Jung writes: "The true man expresses the Anthropos in the individual human being. . . . The true man will destroy no valuable cultural form since he is the highest form of culture. . . ."

From the four cultural attitudes I have described in previous writings, I selected the social attitude as the one best related to the theme of closeness. Religion, aesthetics, and philosophy have important connections with the social origins of culture, so we cannot claim a pure identity for our social attitude. But where the social attitude is present, it holds humankind together in sharing a total experience of cultural identity.

The social attitude was presented in three aspects, personal, cultural, and archetypal. This gives us a method for exploring such attitudes in depth. Starting with the data of ego-consciousness we move into a cultural area that is partly conscious and partly unconscious, thence more deeply into the archetypal area of the collective unconscious where cultural patterns fade into the universal images of human experiences. Such images evoke memories of behavioral adaptations humans have in common with animals, such as the higher apes, as a first configuration of the Anthropos. Because of its psychobiological antiquity this image permeates both cultural and personal areas of awareness. It brings the richness of ancestral tradition up through more recent cultural patterns into the personal lives of all who care to experience a social attitude to its fullest extent. Not all of us need to experience it as a primary attitude; it is sufficient for us to experience it in combination with the other attitudes, religious, aesthetic, and philosophic, provided that they too arise from archetypal depths into the culture in which we feel personally contained.

NOTES

1. Joseph L. Henderson, *Cultural Attitudes in Psychological Perspective* (Toronto: Inner City Books, 1984).
2. Golda Meir, *My Life* (New York, 1975); Lucien Price, *Dialogues with Alfred North Whitehead* (New York); Kenneth Clark, *Another Part of the World: A Self-Portrait* (New York, 1924).
3. Monica Furlong, *Zen Effects: Reflections Leading toward a Unification of Depth Psychology and Physics, The Life of Alan Watts* (Boston: Houghton Mifflin, 1986).
4. Ibid.
5. Marie-Louise von Franz, *Number and Time:* trans. Andrea Dykes (Evanston, Ill.: Northwestern University Press, 1974).
6. Thomas Hobbes, *Leviathan; or, The Matter, Form, and Power of a Commonwealth Ecclesiastical and Civil* (London, 1651).
7. Marie-Louise von Franz, "The Process of Individuation," in *Man and His Symbols* (New York: Doubleday, 1964).

The Many Faces of Closeness

Eleanora M. Woloy

Closeness: "A nearness to anything, or a coming together
to unite, whether the other is another human being, an
animal, nature, God or another layer of oneself."

Today, as the stereotypical roles of men and women
are once again being reexamined, the subject of closeness is particularly relevant. Why? Because ideally, sharing
closeness with another and experiencing curiosity about
our essential differences—without threat—take us beyond
our separateness. Eventually, this leads us to a recognition
of unity where, in truth, men and women are the same.

To approach this subject, I spoke to men and women of
all ages and all walks of life about how they have experienced closeness in their lives. Initially, my sense was that
the capacity for closeness was inherent in the archetypal
feminine principle—that component within the psyche of
humankind that is actively receptive and has the capacity
for imaginal seeing from an all encompassing vantage
point that allows us to be truly present in each moment.
Yet, in choosing to call the capacity for closeness "feminine," I did not wish to perpetuate the use of clichés that
prevent us from moving more deeply into ideas and meaning, or to define the capacity to be vulnerable and open
according to gender. Instead, I believe that closeness is a

human capacity and that both men and women regularly feel closeness and in fact experience it in similar ways.

I particularly want to emphasize this point because of the collective view that to be close, women want to talk and men want to have sex. Recently I saw a cartoon in which a man and a woman sat in opposite chairs, each holding a sign. The man's sign said, "No sex, no love"; the woman's sign said, "No love, no sex." Unfortunately, these stereotypical myths that men and women have about each other do not allow for evolution and growth.

I interviewed twenty men and twenty women for this study. Although some were analysands, the majority were close friends who felt comfortable responding to such a personal question. The aspects of closeness expressed by these people were: something shared; a sudden recognition; an experience often in silence; vulnerability; a sense of freedom; and, for some, a bodily experience. I deeply appreciate all of the people who shared their personal experiences with me.

My intent in conducting these interviews was to look closely at how men and women experience closeness beyond these stereotypes. I asked each person to "describe the feeling of closeness and then tell me about an experience where you experienced this." I was deeply moved by many of the experiences of closeness women described to me, but I have been equally touched by men as I listened to them tell their stories. Although most described connections to other individuals, some described particularly profound connections to nature, animals, or God. Some of the answers carried a common theme, and I have grouped them this way and have purposely not separated the responses of men and women. (The first end note contains a guide as to the gender of each respondent.)[1] I hope reading the responses without this unnecessary discrimination will help you see how I drew my conclusions. Please keep in mind that this is not a statistically validated psychological study but rather my own personal reflections on closeness derived from speaking to women and men and informed by my knowledge of Jungian psychology.

Silence, the experience of being with someone in stillness, without conversation, either sharing the same experience or sharing one's own private experience in the company of another, was a common theme.

1. "To me, closeness means sharing something with another. I remember as a little girl being in a room with my grandmother. She was reading and I was playing. We were both silent, but I remember the feeling of intimacy."

2. "My friend and I would go down to Chapel Hill for supervision and spiritual direction. It would be a long drive and often it was in silence. But the experience of being side by side with my friend was a very good one."

3. "I was dressing one morning, getting ready for work. The doorbell was rung by a man explaining that a dog had been hit by a car on the road in front of my house. He wondered if the dog might be mine. As I wasn't finished dressing, I put on my robe and hurried out to find a small white poodle who had been badly injured. It was not my dog. The man had already knocked at the two other closest homes. He said that he would take the dog to the emergency vet. As I was helping him lift the dog into his car, we looked into each other's faces and for a brief moment, there was the most wonderful feeling of 'knowing.' Not a word was spoken and I never saw the man again."

4. "When my son was eleven, he played baseball and was the pitcher on his team. During a championship game I saw my son call the coach up to the pitcher's mound and tell him that he was too scared to pitch. The coach, undaunted, put him into the outfield and brought in a new pitcher. When the team came in out of the field, I was up against the fence. My son looked at me, and I saw that he had tears in his eyes. I had tears in my eyes, too, and I loved him so much."

5. "Just hours before my sister's death, all pride, all persona, had been stripped away. We were two naked souls faced with the brutality of separation. Knowing that separation was imminent, we did not speak. We trusted love completely. Death had stripped all irrelevancies away so that only supreme love could shine through with no language at all."

6. "When my daughter was born, the scene in the delivery room became like a black-and-white movie. All the equipment, personnel, and walls suddenly disappeared. Everything expanded, and I became intensely focused as the doctor reverently pronounced in a loud whisper, 'It's a girl.' He held her up in triumph, and, at that moment, Jennie, the doctor, God, and I experienced an indescribable harmony."

7. "My friend and I made a fire in the fireplace. I put on some music. Suddenly, there was a dissolution of time and all other people. It seemed as if there was only the light of the fire and the music wrapping around us. It was a deep spiritual experience, and I remember we didn't talk at all although we did make love. But sex wasn't the main thing. It was the timeless being together that I experienced as being so special."

8. "When my father died, my mother asked me, without words, to take over that occasion, which meant

calling relatives from far off all over the country. Speaking to each person who was dear to my mother, knowing I was doing this for her, gave me one of the most profound moments of closeness with her. I was entrusted with being the voice of the family, and she gave that to me. It felt good."

9. "I want to tell an experience of closeness that I witnessed between my daughter and her father. Joyce was about eighteen months old, a little wisp of a girl. She and Al met in the dining room, entering from opposite doorways. I don't know who started it, but their eyes would simultaneously light on a spot on the floor. Without a word, Joyce walked over to a spot, picked up an imaginary feather and would hand it to her daddy. Together they would move their heads following the path of the feather as it floated down to the floor. She would then run to the spot, pick up the feather again and hand it to her daddy. They would repeat this four or five times. What an incredible connection—what fun, what joy."

Sudden recognition was yet another common theme shared by men and women—a sense of a sudden, unexplained feeling of familiarity that led to a feeling of closeness.

1. "In a conversation with another person, there is sometimes a recognition, as if you share something in common. It is a familiar feeling, the recognition of something shared. It is as if a cell in your body ignites and says, 'Boom.' This other is suddenly a part of me too. It is like lighting a candle. A sudden feeling of warmth."

2. "Closeness seems to have a lot to do with the eyes. Somehow it seems as if it is held in the eyes. Sometimes I look at my wife when she is unaware and I see an

expression on her face that she has had for many years, knowing it was the same expression that she had when she was just a little girl. When it happens, I experience such a deep feeling of knowing and continuity that feels very warm and secure."

3. "I need to tell you the feelings that I have for a man. I didn't know why or how I knew he would be special to me. I just knew he was. It seemed like I had found someone I had known before, or like finding a part of yourself that you have tucked away for safekeeping. It was a flash of recognition that said, 'I know you, I have always known you.' It felt like finding the last piece of the puzzle that finally made it complete. The threads of our lives were woven together all in one piece that had a special glow and warmth, a radiance not often seen."

4. "My wife and I were in Zurich. It was time to return home to Canada. We had to decide if my wife would stay in Zurich and finish her analytical work or return home with me. To stay would mean five long years of interruption in our lives. We packed a picnic and went down to Lake Zurich to talk and come to a decision. As we sat on the pier, we could see a man and a woman on the bridge. Suddenly, the man dove off the bridge and the woman began to run. We didn't know if he was trying to commit suicide, or if he was performing some particularly daring feat. We then watched as he began to swim directly to the pier. In the meantime, the woman was running toward us. Just as she reached the pier, he climbed out of the water onto the pier and they both laughed and embraced. My wife and I knew then that she could stay behind and finish her analytical work. We were suddenly aware that we were so close that the time and distance could not separate us."

5. "My greatest experience of closeness occurred when I returned home to see my grandfather after being away for nine months. I knew he was dying. He had changed in those nine months from a strong, vital man to a frail wisp of a man. Knowing I would soon lose him, I was suddenly aware of an intense overwhelming closeness to him."

6. "One day my wife and I were driving down the road. We were arguing about how we would spend our time during this weekend getaway. We were both very angry. In fact, I was so angry that I realized that it was impossible to drive. I pulled the car over to the side of the road. This shocked and surprised my wife. We suddenly both became aware that the love between us was deeper than the temporary anger. We could strip away the unimportant. We felt so close."

7. "When I was nearly twenty and very involved in my church, I decided to become a minister. One evening before a youth rally, the girl to whom I was engaged and I had a serious talk about what it would mean to our lives if I followed my calling. We felt it would involve a life of change and sacrifice. The meeting began, and as I led the prayer, something suddenly came over me. I began to speak words that I had not prepared. My words deeply moved people and they began to come forward to be saved. During this experience, I remember looking up for a moment and catching the eyes of my fiancée. We looked at each other with the sudden, absolute awareness that we were part of something so much bigger than our own personal worries. We felt a deep sense of oneness."

Shared experience, the experience of joining with another in some thought, feeling, or particular action was another common theme.

1. "I come home at night after a long day at work, and when my wife and I finally get to bed, we are both very tired. We know that we are not going to have sex, but I lie on my back with her head on my shoulder and we just talk. It's nice and warm and secure."

2. "Closeness is working together for a common cause, everybody pitching in to get the job done. That's how it is at the office. It's not an attitude of, 'well, this is my job and that is your job.' Instead, we all pitch in for each task that must be done until we get it complete. There is such a shared closeness that we have between us."

3. "For me, closeness is an intense feeling of sharing. Being at oneness. For example, I was at an Elisabeth Kübler-Ross workshop for six days with people I had never met. During those few days, there was a bond like nothing else I have ever experienced. It was the same feeling I had when I was a camp counselor. There was a real closeness among the staff. After a difficult activity that we would complete together, we would feel such closeness."

4. "Closeness is a spontaneous bonding of two people that continues over time, but has moments of feelings of deep inner connections to the other person that occur as the two people share either in a common experience or just simply share their joys, sorrows, and heartaches in a trusting, honest, open way on a deep soul level."

5. "I was involved in a very difficult task for which I felt inadequate. A friend called and when I shared with her that I was having trouble with it, she simply volunteered to be with me. I felt very close to her at that moment because she understood my difficulty."

Vulnerability, a capacity to be open and exposed to another, seemed to be one more component of closeness. Yet, within the experience, it was clear that the sense that one's most tender self had been seen was an important part of this closeness. In fact, this quality of seeing was reflected in William Shakespeare's *King Lear*. In act four, scene six, Lear and Gloucester are on the heath. Although Gloucester has had his eyes put out, he speaks of Lear's situation in a most knowing way. Lear asks, "No eyes in your head, yet you see how this world goes?" Gloucester responds, "I see it feelingly."[2] It is this quality of being "seen" with feelings that allows experiences of vulnerability to be felt as important moments of closeness.

    1. "To feel close, I let someone inside the walls that I usually construct against the outside world. There are no boundaries, no putting out of false images, but it is an experience in which I feel open and I can reach out for more."

    2. "Closeness is a feeling of mutual vulnerability. I had an experience with a woman to whom I was very attracted. She was also attracted to me. We could both acknowledge our desire, knowing that it could not be acted on. It was a mutual wounding, and yet, such joy was felt."

    3. This idea of closeness possibly leading to pain was expressed by another, who stated: "Closeness feels wonderful. Yet, it is scary at the same time. Part of what happens is that I sink down very low, but then I become aware of my own pain in knowing that the other person could hurt or could carry me. It is like a liminal space where there is a sharing but it also includes the pain and I am aware of how I can be hurt."

4. "Last spring I revealed to my wife that our financial situation was very bad. I had been protecting her in attempting to keep up my image of being a good financial manager, but it got beyond me. It was agony to reveal it to her. But it brought me to a place of complete honesty, and there was an awareness that I could be myself, that I did not have to maintain an image and that I did not have to be alone."

5. "My college son and I took a trip in the wilderness. We were on a hike and it was very hot. Although we had planned ahead, we got lost. After some time elapsed, we both began to become dehydrated and felt we were in real danger. Suddenly, it became very clear that we were dependent on each other. When my son began to have trouble walking, I had to help him with his load. Fortunately we made it back to civilization and then my son was able to take over by getting the water. It was a real physical challenge and we experienced an amazing sense of closeness through our sense of dependence upon each other."

6. "In closeness there seems to be a sense of neediness involved. I can feel close to a person when they reveal a neediness, or if they 'own' their own neediness. I remember a time when a friend and I were hugging. Suddenly, we realized that we were hugging from the waist up. We both laughed and were able to give each other a real, full body hug."

Freedom, the power to determine one's own action, seemed to be another quality that was expressed by a number of individuals.

1. "To me, closeness feels like a state of contentment. When I am with another person, we are contained and yet relaxed. Each of us is free to move. When I feel this closeness with a man, it is translated into a sense of

passion. Yet, there is a trusting of the other to give to me without possession. It is a sharing with an open hand. Not possessiveness. It's like dancing, each person moving in a different direction, yet, in harmony. Closeness is a gifting of yourself with no return expected."

2. "I used to play competitive sports. There was a real team bonding, a closeness between the guys on the team. We depended on each other and thus, were vulnerable to each other. We could feel close, and yet, if one of the guys left the team, it was OK. There was no sticky attachment."

3. "To me closeness occurs in the experience of having sex with a partner where no further commitment is expected. It allows me the freedom to be close."

It is interesting that many people talked about closeness as a direct experience of the *body*. It seems to be a deep bodily response that allows us to move out of our normal time frame into circular rather than linear time with a heightened sense of vulnerability and knowing, yet the freedom to not become lost in the experience.

1. "I feel closeness in my body. I feel as if I have no skin. There is a deep connection but I don't feel overwhelmed. I don't feel swallowed up by the other."

2. "Closeness is the ability to touch and be touched without a sexual connotation. I feel totally free in myself and that sense of openness by the other person's touching me."

3. "Closeness is felt in the body. It is as if I recognize something in a body that makes me feel close."

4. "Closeness feels like a warm place. It is as if I and the other person are in a bubble together. I physically experience the other person, feeling the heat of the body

or the emotional heat of the experience. There seems to be a slowing down of time almost as if time didn't matter at all. There is a sense that there is no struggle to do anything, no effort. I remember the time when I was with my girlfriend and we were wandering down the street just shopping and walking with a deep sense of excitement. Everything was possible. There was a timelessness and a security. There was no effort, but a deep sense of being known and knowing the other person. There was a sense of oneness, but also a separateness. Merging but stepping out and then merging again at will, without fear. All self-consciousness was gone."

Several individuals described their closest experiences as deep feelings in connection to nature or as a oneness with *nature* and *God.*

1. "Celebration of the Eucharist is my deepest feeling of closeness. The most wonderful food, to touch it and give it makes me connected to people and to God."

2. "My brother and I went to the cemetery to visit our mother and father's grave. Since the gates of the cemetery were locked, we just stood outside looking at the gravestones, which were close enough to the gate so that we could see them. It was a cloudy day. Suddenly as we were standing there, the sun appeared and hit the granite on my father's gravestone. It began to shine with a golden glow. As we stood there, the sun moved and the glow continued over my mother's gravestone. This was a highly spiritual moment. I felt the warmth of sharing that experience with my brother. There they were—our two parents in the glow of the sun and the two children who honored them. We reflected the warmth. We were very grateful."

3. "One day last week, I was riding my stationary bike. I had decided to take the twenty minutes to listen

to angelic music and do my centering prayer and let whatever images come. Suddenly, I had an image of a womb. It felt like it was Mother God's womb and I was in it. I was close to everything—all people, all creatures, all nature. It was the first time I felt the life force and energy in things I used to call 'inanimate.' "

4. "Closeness feels to me like there are no boundaries, no I and Thou—just delight. A mystical experience. Feeling the true livingness of earth and air and water. Feeling the joy in a kitten, in a baby, or in an old person's wrinkles."

5. "I was walking through the woods on a beautiful sunny day in late April. It was still cool, but the sun was very warm. I found a place behind a rock out of the wind and I took off my clothes and laid them on the leaves and lay down. When I began to feel the warmth of the sun on my entire body, I had an orgasmic experience feeling united with the sun, the trees above me, and the earth on which I lay. It was a deep feeling of passionate closeness to all."

6. "Closeness feels warm and comfortable. I remember lying on the floor taking a nap, when my dog came up and gently rested her head on my body. I had deep feelings of closeness to her and to the world."

To further explore the meaning of closeness, consider the etymology of the word. "Close" is derived from the Latin verb *claudo,* meaning to "close a container; to surround with a boundary; enclose; to include or embrace with a limit."[3] The word is also related to the Greek noun *kleis,* meaning a catch or hook passed through the door from the outside; or a sacred key. Although a key locks and closes a door, which reflects the notion of limit, it also opens a door. This suggests the sense of openness that is necessary to experience closeness. The Greek meaning also includes "a rowing bench in a ship."[4] This is reminiscent of shoulder-to-shoulder, or side-by-side as experienced by one of the individuals whom I interviewed. The Sanskrit root *klein* or *kleu* means close; key; cloister; to hook; a lot, lotto, lottery.[5] Thus perhaps the gamble of closeness is reflected by the idea of vulnerability or opening oneself to the possibility of hurt.

My sense of the meaning of closeness from these root words is that it carries the feeling of being enclosed. There is a sense of people being together with a boundary around them, enclosed by their shared experience. Yet another reflection of the language that conveys the meaning of closeness is contained within the American Sign Language, which uses four different hand signs to communicate the experience: the sign for side-by-side, or proximity; the sign for a best friend (not just friend but best friend); the sign for sweethearts; and the sign to indicate mental telepathy or the capacity to read each other's minds. This is another indication of the many levels of connection that closeness implies.

Primarily, the reflections of closeness involved another person, but in some instances they involved a closeness to God and nature and, in fact, all creation. For the most part, each of the responses focused on the specific qualities of closeness that I outlined and these qualities were shared equally by women and men. However, it was interesting to note that the quality of vulnerability was present in the responses of five males and only one female. And the experience of closeness to God, nature, or all creation was experienced by five women and only one man. This seems particularly noteworthy since for the quality of "vulnerability" to be an important aspect of closeness for more men than women would seem to indicate that men feel "at risk" in a situation of closeness.

A hypothesis has been suggested by Carol Gilligan to explain the distinct characteristics that men and women acquire.[6] First, there is the notion that since women play the key parental role and act as the focus of the life of infants and children, boys have to distinguish themselves from the mother and separate from her to identify themselves with "maleness." Girls do not have to make this separation. Because of the early developmental sequences, women have a tendency toward relationships in their psyches while men develop a tendency toward separation of self.

Another idea suggests that gender identity is social rather than psychic, as the first theory implies. This suggests the theory that our identity is learned from the many ways boys and girls are taught and expected to act through both direct teaching and from the internalization of the model of gender as experienced in the world around us.

I feel that both theories figure into our development of gender identity. And, since it is clear that our psychic and social structures do not promote vulnerability in men, this quality is of greater importance to them. What's more, I feel that to be open to another person implies surrender and trust, which is difficult for everyone—particularly for men who have received the messages by our culture that to be strong, brave, and not to cry is to be masculine.

In addition, because inclusive, relational qualities are intrinsic to the psyches of women, it is easier for them to talk of their connection to God and the universe. Also, it seems to me that women are given more permission to be able to talk of mystical experiences. Each of the men in the study except the one who spoke of the closeness to his dog gave responses that were in relation to another person.

As an analyst, I have had the opportunity to explore the psyches of many men with whom I work, and I know that men, too, experience this deep connection with the universe. It is therefore particularly interesting that only one man gave a direct reference to a sexual experience as his example of closeness. In our culture men are not encouraged to discuss their feelings, and all too often sex becomes the outlet for feelings. My findings indicate that this does not mean that closeness for men is only experienced as "sex," only that for some men this may be the most acceptable means of discussing the subject. It is not known whether subjects' responses were gender-related to the questioner.

I began this study with the premise that closeness is a human experience felt by both men and women in similar ways. The responses indicated that this premise is correct. The experience of "closeness" almost always involved another—whether another human being, an animal, or God and the universe. In addition, it seems to be an experience that has boundaries and seems to enclose the individuals involved. It also involves openness and sharing. The basis of this premise is grounded more in terms of the process of closeness rather than linguistics.

I believe the capacity for closeness is a relatedness that proceeds not from the ego or any individual archetype, but rather from the inner central organizing archetype of the psyche, the Self.

In *Projection and Re-Collection in Jungian Psychology,* Marie-Louise von Franz discusses at length the relationship between relatedness or closeness and the individuation process. The first stage of individuation is the unification of the personality. This is the work of separating our own personal myth from the family myth and discovering the hidden parts of our personality so that we are indeed living more closely in line with our whole and unique nature. The second stage, according to von Franz, involves the relatedness to one's fellow human beings and to mankind as a whole. It is not only the relationship between parts of oneself that is contained within the union of the Self, but it is the many other relationships with one's fellow creatures. "Bonds with other people are produced by the Self and these relations are very exactly regulated as to distance and closeness. One might describe this as the social function of the Self. Each person gathers around himself or herself his or her own soul family. Whereas relations based merely on projection are characterized by fascination and dependence, this kind of relationship by way of the Self has something strictly objective, strangely transpersonal about it. It gives rise to a feeling of immediate timeless being together."[7]

In his autobiography, Carl Jung wrote, "Objective cognition lies hidden behind the attraction of the emotional relationship; it seems to be the central secret."[8] Objective cognition is the capacity to be aware of another without projection, transference, or fantasy—it is a direct soul-to-soul connection.

On April 18, 1941, Jung wrote in a letter to Mary Mellon that in a world created by the Self, we meet all those many to whom we belong—those whose hearts we touch. "Here," he continues, "there is no distance but immediate presence. It is the eternal secret—how shall I ever explain it?"[9] This beautiful statement of objective cognition is reminiscent of the young woman who said to me, "In a conversation with another person, there is sometimes a recognition, as if you share something in common. It is a familiar feeling, the recognition of something shared. It is as if a cell in your body ignites and says

'Boom.' This other is suddenly a part of me too. It's like lighting a candle, a sudden feeling of warmth."

There is a place in each of us, more primal and more spiritual than words can convey, that seems to be the source of our capacity to experience closeness. The Self, the central dynamism of the personality, does contain polarities such as masculine and feminine principles with very specific qualities. But I believe that the ability to share closeness comes, not from one of the poles, but from the central unifying archetype within all of us. Thus we each have the capacity for sharing and in the sharing, we are transformed.

NOTES

1. *Silence:* (1) F, (2) M, (3) F, (4) M, (5) F, (6) F, (7) M, (8) M, (9) F. *Sudden Recognition:* (1) F, (2) M, (3) F, (4) M, (5) M, (6) M, (7) M. *Shared Experience:* (1) M, (2) F, (3) M, (4) F, (5) F. *Vulnerability:* (1) F, (2) M, (3) M, (4) M, (5) M, (6) M. *Freedom:* (1) F, (2) M, (3) M. *Body:* (1) F, (2) F, (3) F, (4) M. *God and Nature:* (1) F, (2) F, (3) F, (4) F, (5) F, (6) M.

2. Howard Staunton, ed., *The Complete Illustrated Shakespeare* (New York: Park Lane, 1979).

3. P. G. W. Clase, ed., *The Oxford Latin Dictionary* (Oxford: Oxford University Press, 1968).

4. Henry G. Liddell and Robert Scott, *Greek-English Lexicon* (Oxford: Oxford University Press, 1968).

5. Joseph T. Shipley, *The Origins of English Words* (Baltimore: Johns Hopkins University Press, 1984).

6. Carol Gilligan, *In a Different Voice* (Cambridge: Harvard University Press, 1982), pp. 160–163.

7. Marie-Louise von Franz, *Projection and Re-Collection in Jungian Psychology* (London: Open Court, 1978), p. 177.

8. C. G. Jung, *Memories, Dreams, Reflections.* Recorded and

edited by Aniela Jaffé; translated by Richard and Clara Winston (New York and London: Vintage Books, 1961), p. 297.

9. Jung, *Letters,* vol. 1. Selected and edited by Gerhard Adler and Aniela Jaffé (Princeton, N.J.: Princeton University Press, 1973 and 1975), p. 298.

Son of a Psychiatrist

Thomas Wilmer

One of the earliest labels attached to me was "son of a psychiatrist." I'm forty-one years old now, and so far the label has stuck like glue. I suspect that it will stick until I die.

I was one of four rambunctious and demonstrative brothers, and we had one sister. We constituted an ipso facto gang of sorts. When any five wild and active kids get together, I can guarantee you some social interactions that would make any civilized adult cringe. If the behavior is explained by saying, "You know, their father is a *psychiatrist*," then everything begins to make sense and is somehow excusable in the affronted party's mind.

I remember hearing family friends and acquaintances excuse away my and my siblings' animated activities with similar comments as early as kindergarten. By sixth grade, I had heard the old axiom, "All psychiatrists' kids are crazy, messed up, or screwed up," so many times that somewhere deep inside, I must have known it to be fact.

As I grew older, the albatross clung tightly to my chest. I'd find myself on a perfectly even plateau with the next guy, until it was mentioned or revealed that I was *the son of a psychiatrist*. Then came the point-blank question or statement regarding my presumed instability or probable insanity.

We grew up in the heyday of Dr. Benjamin Spock. To compound our situation, my father was a personal friend of the good doctor. If an excuse for my behavior couldn't be pinned directly on the well-documented childhood disease of "sonofapsych-itis," the next best scapegoat was my father's *presumed* zealot-like implementation of Dr. Spock's directives as set forth in his 1946 classic parenting bible, *Baby and Child Care*. The "son-of-a-psychiatrist" label, and its repeated reinforcement, led me to question seriously my own sanity and that of others about me. I noticed that when other children misbehaved, they were just "kids being kids." I, on the other hand, who misbehaved in exactly the same way, heard the demeaning and sometimes cruel explanation that I was "screwed up" because of *you know what*.

Many times I felt like screaming, "*What?* It's not true. I'm me and my actions are mine in spite of what my father does for a living. I bet if my dad were a janitor, I'd still do the same crazy things!"

Over the years, I learned to tell people that my father is "a medical doctor with a concentration in neurology and a Ph.D. in pathology who subsequently went on to specialize in Jungian psychotherapy." This description resulted in different reactions from when I said merely, "He's a psychiatrist."

The longer introduction tends to diffuse the potent stereotypes associated with psychiatry. To this day, at times, I will introduce my father with the longer and disarming description of his current specialization.

Just last week, a "professional" friend inquired, "Is it true that all shrinks' kids are screwed up?" "Yeah," I replied, "just like everyone else."

I read the previous paragraph to my girlfriend, and she said, "Well of course. Everyone knows that psychiatrists' kids are screwed up. There's definitely a higher proportion of screwed up kids among children of psychiatrists."

"*What?*" I asked incredulously. "Just where do you get your statistics?" She responded, "Well, I guess it's an unfair accusation because my opinion is limited to the offspring of psychiatrists that I've known personally." Suddenly, I found myself questioning my own sanity again. Her reaction amazed me. I thought, "How could a well-educated instructor of biology and life science harbor such blind stereotypes?" Then a voice in my mind said, "Well, if the sum total of her acquaintants, who are offspring of psychs, are messed up, isn't that a pretty good random sample? Doesn't that prove her statement correct?"

Feed a fever, send the kid to the child psychiatrist for a "cold." When I was young, I assumed that most people thought anyone seeing a psychiatrist must be crazy, still a somewhat common assumption among the public, I believe. What is one of the first things that investigators look for when they're out to discredit a politician seeking office? Evidence of previous psychiatric care. Even a brush with a shrink twenty long years ago is enough to knock the wind out of a political campaign. The politician will scramble to explain the particulars for weeks to come.

Unfortunately, at times, for a psychiatrist's child, shrinks often avidly boost their craft. My father attempted to work with me and my childhood problems, but as he once said, "You know, it's sad, but it's the hardest for me to help the people closest to me." So off I was sent to one of his colleagues, a child psychiatrist.

When I think back on my childhood, I picture myself being sent to the child psychiatrist as readily as the child of an internist is sent to the family general practitioner for a cold or sore throat. It was as if my father believed that psychiatry was "good for what ails you."

I don't think I actually went all *that* often, but due to the stigma of seeing a "kiddie head shrinker," I remember these visits much more distinctly than those to the family practitioner. By the fifth grade, I was street-smart enough to tell friends that "I was just at the doctor's," and avoided the topic of the "shrink" altogether.

The simple revision of two labels helped liberate me from the negative associations with my father's profession. The most powerful change occurred when I learned that my father was no longer a Freudian. He had undergone a lengthy period of Freudian analysis during the early 1950s when I was in the midst of my most vulnerable psychosocial formative years.

I hated the negative sexual categorizing and labeling of people's problems. In my eyes, Freudian training seemed to arm the therapist with convenient but potentially dangerous preconceptions of the working of others' minds. It was as if therapists were out there presumptuously searching for little cracks in people's armor. When they looked at the mind, they inevitably found a Freudian concept of some sort manifesting itself. I will never forget my earliest and most alarming encounter with "off-the-wall" Freudianism at work.

When I was in kindergarten, my father took me out to a favorite hamburger stand at Menlo Park for lunch one afternoon. After we finished, we piled into his green 1952 Chevrolet convertible. He pulled onto El Camino Real and moments later, when he stopped for a red light, he turned and asked me one of the most mystifying questions I've ever been asked. We had been discussing what he understood to be some of my academic and socialization problems at school. Then he inquired therapeutically, "Do you ever have fears of having your penis cut off?"

"No!" I answered.

I found the concept completely foreign. To me, my little penis was just another appendage—no different from one of my arms or legs. I had never thought of losing an arm or leg, let alone a penis. Maybe I had exhibited some behavior that made my dad pursue that line of questioning. I only know that I had never before consciously thought anything remotely like that. I found the question so bizarre that I still remember it clearly. Later, I assumed that this question and others that were alien to my thinking were by-products of his Freudian training and his analytic instructors.

When I first learned that my father had become a Jungian analyst, I was elated. By association, I suddenly felt free from Freud and his obsession with negative sexual explanations for dreams, actions, and behavior.

To me, Freud was definitely the shadow, obsessive, gloomy, dark and brooding, an autocratic pigeonholer. Jung was a bright ray of early morning sunshine bursting upon the scene. Jung represented hope, possibilities, options, and one's right to take responsibility for one's own emotions and actions.

It was wonderful to be able to say with pride, "My dad is a Jungian," after mumbling for so long, "I think he follows Freud, but he's really eclectic in his theories. He also follows Carl Rogers, Adler, and others."

The second and more general change occurred when a concerted decision was made (by, I assume, the American Psychiatric Association or some other organization) to address "mental illness" as "mental health." It had a cleansing and purifying effect. It was refreshing to be able to say, "My mom works at the community mental *health* building," rather than "My mom works at the community mental *illness* building." It was only a word change, but what a powerful inversion of perception it was.

Even though much of my behavior probably would have been the same if my father had been a janitor, major parts of who I am were dictated by his profession and professionalism.

He was a boy with a mission. As a twelve-year-old, he constructed an elaborate scale-model hospital, complete to the last-minute detail. He knew who he was to be when he was very young. He was driven by overbearing parents and his own consuming inner drive and curiosity.

He whipped through an undergraduate program in three years and medical school in three years. His appetite for research was so voracious that he picked up a Ph.D. without even knowing it. Someone suggested that he apply for a doctorate in pathology. When he investigated the requirements necessary for the degree, he was informed that he merely had to take a course in French and the degree was his since he had already published more than six scientific papers under his name.

A licensed physician at the age of twenty-three, he was forced to grow a mustache so that patients would take him seriously. By the age of twenty-five, he had written and illustrated the first of his many published books. By the time he was forty years old, Hollywood was knocking at his door with an offer to produce a television special on the pioneering work he did in social psychiatry while running a naval psychiatric ward for Korean War vets.

His friendships with such powerful figures as Hubert Humphrey, Admiral Chester W. Nimitz, Ben Spock, and Lee Marvin compounded his bigger than life image in my eyes.

I found my father and his accomplishments quite overwhelming and intimidating, to say the least. When I was in high school, people repeatedly asked me if I was going to become a physician and psychiatrist. When I answered no, they then asked if my father was hurt and let down because of my failure to follow in his footsteps.

I suspect that if my dad had been a janitor, my fear of failure would have been greatly mitigated. I am grateful that he didn't pressure or dictate my choice of profession. Instead, he provided ample indirect stimulus for me to become interested in science and the healing arts.

When I was in the third grade, he was working at Mayo Clinic in Rochester, Minnesota. He would sometimes take me with him to the hospital when he was scheduled for rounds. He'd grab a cloth surgical mask, tie it around my nose and mouth, and escort me into the balcony of an operating room. And there he'd leave me to watch the surgeons below perform major surgery while he went off on his rounds.

The surgery balcony made a convenient baby-sitter, but I have not the slightest doubt that my father hoped I'd be struck by the powerful magic of medicine while I watched the healing hands of the surgeons below. When I was a sixth-grader, he arranged for me to spend an afternoon with a Stanford University pioneer in electron microscopy. Later I spent time with Professor Wolfe of the University of Texas at San Antonio, one of the country's foremost researchers in sleep, and with researchers in the university's biofeedback laboratory. I also spent an afternoon with a neurosurgeon as he conducted exploratory diagnostic tests on patients.

My father said, "Yes, I would be pleased if you became a physician or a Jungian, but what I want most is for you to be content in whatever you choose."

I think he wanted to spare me from the parental pressures he suffered, yet he couldn't resist the temptation to at least unlock and open every door in my path.

He gave me the freedom to choose my own route through life. After foundering for a few years, I told him how frustrated I was due to too many choices. He laughed. "Yes, freedom is a prison in many ways," he said.

I find myself measuring my life against my father's. When I turned twenty-three, I asked myself, "Where's your medical degree?" At twenty-five, I asked, "Well, where's your book?" And on and on.

When I was very young, I learned that my father was a social psychiatrist. I understood the word *social* to be synonymous with "society at large." As a first-grader, I was aware that he was in charge of a ward full of battle-fatigued Korean War veterans. I knew that the mental health of those soldiers was of paramount concern to him.

Later, when he was working with San Quentin convicts, I also understood what sacrifices he had made to help this society of people. I knew that his financial remuneration for his efforts was equal to a prison guard's salary. I also knew that some San Francisco Bay Area private practitioners were knocking down the astounding sum of seventy-five or even a hundred dollars per hour—and that was twenty-five years ago.

At a very early age, I clearly perceived that my father had made personal and family sacrifices for the betterment of mankind. This perception allowed me to defer a lot of personal needs for closeness with my father. I witnessed his exhilaration when one of his projects won accolades from colleagues or a new concept proved successful.

As I matured and my needs became more complex, my confusion about life overwhelming, I thought I could turn to the Wunderkind of the mind—my father—for answers.

By the time I was in high school, he was working long and obsessive hours at the University of California, San Francisco, topped off by a grueling commute down the peninsula to our Palo Alto home. Usually he'd arrive toward the end of dinner or later. He'd grab a bite to eat and sail on out to his office in the converted garage. There he'd stay, typing away on his IBM Selectric until past midnight.

The counterculture, the war in Vietnam, and drugs were the consuming subjects of the time, and I needed answers badly. I'd slither out to his office late at night, hoping that he would stop to visit. I'd knock. He'd wheel around in his red fabric-covered office chair, smile, and ask what was up. I'd say, "Can I come in and talk?" He'd say encouragingly, "Sure, come on in and have a seat. I'll be with you in a moment." I took the word "moment" literally. While waiting for his moment to elapse, I would first memorize all the book titles on the shelf. After reading the current issue of the *Journal of the American Medical Association*, I'd rustle the pages to get his attention.

Finally, he'd swing around in his chair, smile, and ask, "What's on your mind?" I would swear he had no idea that a long half hour had passed. He acted as if I had just sat on the couch a moment before. Sometimes I just wanted to talk about *anything*, the subject was of no consequence. I just wanted to connect with him.

Sometimes I'd open up and ramble on about what was bugging me. When I stopped, he would say, "Hmmmmm," or "What do you think?" then take a puff on his pipe. I didn't want a "Hmmmmm"; I wanted a brilliantly delivered plan of action and answers to my thoughts and problems. I had assumed that the "great doctor" had all the answers. I didn't know it at the time, but he was teaching me to find my own answers. What's the deal with this guy? I thought. He's the great communicator, the wordsmith, the person who, I thought, "talked" to people for fifty minutes at a stretch, all day long. When I mention the phenomenon to friends whose parents are psychiatrists, they laugh and add their own version of the parent who perpetually responded, "Hmmmmm," to their communications.

Late one night in 1968, I reached out for help and discovered a paradox. I was seventeen; it was the "Summer of Love"; Haight Ashbury was in full bloom. Gray Line buses, loaded with tourists from places like Peoria, made daily excursions through the kingdom of the hippies. Many in my generation viewed LSD and marijuana as important tools for unlocking the doors to the unconscious and for expanding the mind. I began my own experimentation with drugs. I needed answers. Although I knew the potential for disaster associated with drugs, drugs were enticing nevertheless.

I decided to ask my father about the various drugs and about the rumors that LSD can cause chromosomal damage. While I waited, I listened to his typewriting clacking. In the background, an opera singer warbled from the radio. He finally found a convenient stopping place and turned toward me. He responded to my questions with short, specific, and direct answers. He then apologized profusely and said that he would have to get back to his writing since he was on some sort of deadline.

The punchline is that his paper dealt with the research ward he operated at UCSF's Langley Porter neuropsychiatric teaching hospital. The name of the project that had consumed his every waking hour? "Youth Drug Study Ward."

I vowed to avoid the trap of becoming too busy for my child. Yet as I sat writing, my daughter came in and asked a question. "Not right now, Celena," I replied. "I'm in the middle of something." After she left the room, I felt this stab in my side. I find myself in many ways perpetuating, on an entirely different scale, my father's behaviors.

In my own realm, I feel successful. I own a general contracting business. I'm the travel editor of a local paper, a freelance contributor to other publications, the travel correspondent and a board member of the National Public Radio affiliate serving Santa Barbara and San Luis Obispo counties. I'm also a photographer and illustrator. The other day, my daughter confided to my girlfriend that she had been hostile toward me because my multifaceted activities and accomplishments intimidated her and made her feel inadequate. I was stunned. All this time, I had been discounting my own accomplishments because I still compare myself with my father and still feel inadequate. All the time, my daughter had been feeling the very same thing in relation to me.

I cherish my early, formative years with my father. For a while, there were only three of us, until the other two children came. Three are a lot more manageable than five. He took time to play with us. He built us forts, tire swings, jungle gyms, merry-go-rounds, taught us to box, and wrestled with us on the floor.

One of the most precious things that he did was turn my older brothers' room into a ship. By the door was a painted nameplate that proclaimed the room the *S.S. Hankjohn*. He had scoured the local army-navy surplus store for nautical paraphernalia. On one wall was a ship's wheel. Nearby was a porthole with a fish tank behind. He rigged up a periscope and speaking tubes mined from some old destroyer, and added numerous other details.

Sadly, the older we got, and the more of us there were,

the busier he became. His career and the demands upon his professional time skyrocketed. The residual time for family correspondingly decreased.

At least we had some superb early moments of closeness and bonding. But the instinctual need for fatherly contact never diminished in any of us, nor did my father's desire to spend quality time with each of us.

On most of his speaking tours to medical societies or conventions, he'd rotate through the ranks and take one of us along. He made time for us, one way or another. Sometimes we accompanied him on his Saturday house calls, or when he drove up to see his patients in the Belmont Sanitarium. But I have no recollection of a camping, hunting, or fishing trip with my father beyond the age of nine.

When I was in junior high school, I desperately wanted to go camping with my dad, but the chance never came. I know he, too, was desperate for such a trip, but his commitments precluded that from happening. I found my own substitutes for my father in my friends' fathers and in older acquaintances. Fortunately, I was independent enough to fill the void I felt with work and play.

I still felt cheated out of something that many of my friends, whose parents were not physicians or psychiatrists, experienced in junior and senior high school.

When I was fourteen, out of the blue, my dad invited me to go fishing with him. For years I had waited for such a proposition. Finally, he was reaching out to touch me. I said no. I thought, but didn't say, "It's too late, Dad!" I sensed his panic over the belief that this was his last chance to bond with the boy. He faced that moment when a parent realizes, "My God, my child is almost grown and gone. Why it seems like I was cradling him in my arms just yesterday." I saw that in his face; I saw it for exactly what it was, yet I still cruelly rebuked his heartfelt offer and coldly said, "No." Damn, I wanted to cry then. I feel like crying now.

I know my dad was as desperate to do "family" things as we children were. The realization that there had been too little too late must have been excruciating for him. I know that, as I watch my own daughter grow up, blindingly fast, right before my eyes, and I find myself deferring things that cannot be deferred. I feel my father's anguish, my own and my daughter's.

Even as late as my high school years, I thought my father was endowed with X-ray vision. His attentive eyes would pierce me, and I knew he could see deep into my soul or at least read my subconscious thoughts. I wished for a lead shield to block his exfoliating abilities.

Because I believed he could read my mind, I made some confessions I might otherwise have avoided. Later I learned that he was no better at mind reading than anyone else.

I was fortunate in his handling of my dreams. When I shared a dream with him, he would usually prod out of me my own interpretation of the symbolism. A close friend of mine was not so lucky. His father was a psychiatrist in Scotland. One morning at the breakfast table, he told his dad a dream he'd had the previous night. "Hmmmmm," his father said. Then he stated that his son's dream was "a manifestation of a reverse Oedipal complex. . . . You harbor deep-seated thoughts of wanting to kill both of your parents." My friend said, "That was the one and only time I ever tried to share one of my dreams with him!"

For years, I saw my father as a man with the wisdom of a sage, as a social scientist with a crystal-clear perception of groups, subgroups, and the individual, as an omnipotent judge and an oracle of sorts. My older brother John offered me my first glimpse of his fallibility. John, who had a somewhat abrasive relationship with our father, had always believed that "the old man" didn't sit any higher than the rest of us. Almost in passing, John mentioned a book written by the father of one of our father's patients on the "Youth Drug Study Ward" at UCSF. The book contained a passage about my father that was not at all flattering. John shoved the book in my face and showed me the damning lines. He then told me how much the critical comments had hurt Dad. I was momentarily stunned. How dare this man, with only the slightest knowledge of who my father was or what he thought, say such cruel things? Before long, I realized that it was merely one man's opinion. Most important, I began to realize that many psychiatrists, psychologists, social workers, and nurses in the world would question and oppose anything and everything that my father might say or write. At this point in my life, I also began to understand that a certain percentage of people will always hold positions contrary to the remainder.

Part of the reason I saw my father as a wise old sage was his pensive and brooding expressions. Often he looked like a man deep in thought. It wasn't until I was almost eighteen that I began to see some of his distant and quiet moods for what they were—good old depression. He had finally confided to me, in very clear terms, the burden he carried home from eight or ten hours of listening to his patients' convoluted and torturous problems. I had always perceived him as a man of steel. I had thought he had invincible walls that defended him from the infectiousness of his patients' thoughts. When I began to understand and appreciate the weight of his load, I gained a strong empathy for this man whose job Sisyphus could have recognized.

If my father could travel back in time and take one more run at life with me there to counsel him as a fellow adult, I'd probably actually advise him to go the same course all over again. But I would recommend one simple change. I would say to him, and to all analysts with children, "Smell the roses, Grasshopper!" Take a little more time out along the way.

Closeness in Personal Relationship

Mary Ann Mattoon

In a popular song from the musical comedy *South Pacific* we are told that "some enchanted evening" someone will appear "across a crowded room." The song goes on to identify the stranger as one's "true love" and implies lifelong happiness with that stranger if the impulse is followed to "fly to her side and make her your own." If one does not act in this way, "all through your life you will dream all alone." The song states that no one can explain such a situation: "Fools give you reasons; wise men never try." At the risk of playing the fool, I shall suggest a reason and an alternative way of dealing with the situation.

To many people, making such a stranger "one's own" constitutes a personal "relationship." For Jung and Jungians, personal relationship is a broader concept—and a narrower one. It is broader in including a variety of models, not just the "sexual model" of lovers (married, committed, or neither); it is narrower in requiring a degree of consciousness that is often lacking in a sexual liaison.

The models of association include also those of child-parent, siblings, friends, teacher-student, employer-employee, and coworkers. ("Association" subsumes all forms and levels of personal connection.) All these models have the potential to achieve what Jung called "psychological relationship."

Sexual attraction may be present in any such association but, except for lovers (male-female and same-sex), is not acted out. If the sexual attraction is acted out by pairs other than those composed of consenting peers, the relationship is violated, perhaps destroyed.

Expressions such as "falling in love" and "love is blind" reflect the unconsciousness that is likely to accompany sexual attraction. "Love at first sight" (the kind of "love" described in the song) is a synonym for projecting a content necessary to one's own wholeness onto another person and falling in love with that. Such projection is an unconscious phenomenon. We do not create it; it happens to us.

A psychological relationship, in the Jungian view, is an association that starts with a large component of assumption (because on first meeting one has little information about the other person) but attains a degree of consciousness. Such a relationship is based on an emotional bond that is strong enough to be satisfying and to be worth the difficulties that arise and the pain that ensues. The satisfactions of psychological relationship include giving—emotionally and probably in other ways—as well as receiving. Indeed, giving and receiving cease to be separate processes. The parties in the relationship experience the grace of sharing, with energy moving in both directions. Another word for such a connection is *love*.

MODELS OF RELATIONSHIP

Our experience with our parents is the ground of our humanness. They or their substitutes are necessary for our survival—through physical and emotional nurturing, helping us to discover the world, instructing us in matters that are not amendable to direct discovery. Other adults in a child's life—neighbors, relatives, teachers—may fill some of the parental role.

For a time a newborn child probably exists in a state of identification with the nurturing person, usually the mother. This identification is an important stage but is not yet a relationship. As Jung pointed out, "In order to be conscious of myself, I must be able to distinguish myself from others. Relationship can only take place where this distinction exists."[1]

Authoritarian parents have only a limited relationship with their children, as do parents whose lives are sacrificed completely to their children's wishes. In a psychological relationship between parent and child, the shared decision-making grows as the child gains in life experience.

Another model of relationship is that of siblings. Brothers and sisters, like parents, are given to us; they are not of our choosing. We may value them as the companions of our childhood. We also may compete with them and fight with them, to distinguish ourselves as individuals. Often, true psychological relationship between siblings occurs only in adulthood, when they become equals and are no longer primarily competitors or seen as older or younger than each other.

Friendship, a third model, is likely to be the first relationships of one's own choosing. It may start with a chance connection, such as with another child who lives in the neighborhood and becomes one's playmate. These associations may become relationships as they continue to develop through the school years, often characterized by common backgrounds or interests, but based on mutual liking and affection. In adult life a friendship may be based on a common interest, such as parenthood of young children, and pass into history when that interest is no longer operative. A limited number of friendships develop that are based on deep mutual appreciation and trust. A very few may last throughout the life span.

As we begin to move away from the family, we may find persons—contemporaries or elders—who become our teachers and mentors. As we participate in school, religious institutions and clubs, these persons instruct us about the world. Later we may find mentors who teach and encourage us in establishing ourselves as adults. (A neighbor or relative may be a combination of parent, friend, and mentor.) A teacher/mentor may pass out of one's life when that function is needed no longer, or that person may become a friend.

The employer-employee association has the special difficulty of the difference in economic power; the employee's financial condition and status in the world are at stake. Nevertheless, it is possible for some relationship to develop out of openness and honesty about the issues that arise in working together.

With coworkers there is an economic bond; we depend on one another for the stability of our livelihood. We also share a common task to which we may be deeply committed. This relationship usually includes mutual support, learning skills from each other, exchanging the gossip of the workplace. Such an association may continue beyond the time of shared work. If so, it takes on characteristics of another model, usually friendship, but perhaps parent-child or teacher-student.

Eventually we assume the role(s) of parent, teacher, mentor, and/or employer in newer associations, often with younger people.

Each model may be personified in more than one person. For example, a teacher or Scout leader can fill some of the parental role to a young male; a woman friend can be, at times, a teacher to another woman. In marriage the spouses play various roles for each other: parent, teacher, friend, as well as sexual and economic partner. A therapist is likely to fill some of the role of parent and also of mentor.

All these associations can produce emotional bonds and may result in psychological relationships.

JUNG AND JUNGIANS ON CLOSENESS AND RELATIONSHIP

I see *closeness* as a synonym for psychological relationship. Virtually identical with closeness is "intimacy," emotional and/or sexual.

Not every interpersonal association, however frequent the contacts, qualifies as a relationship. But if the participants have some self-understanding and are willing to pay the price, the association can become close and truly psychological.

The capacity for relatedness—a percursor to relationship—is a generally human quality. Jung called it "eros" and saw it as "feminine," while specifying that it is essential for the wholeness of both females and males.

Like other psychological theorists, Jung did not question the importance of relationship for human survival and well-being, physical and emotional. He had most to say, however, about the integral role of relationship in psychological development. His own work focused on male-female peer relationships and, to a lesser degree, on parent-child relationships.

The importance of psychological development does not mean that Jung saw relationship as arising out of strength. Indeed, he wrote in his late years, "A human relationship

. . . is based . . . on imperfection, on what is weak, helpless and in need of support—the very ground and motive for dependence."[2] Acceptance of weakness, in ourselves and others, is essential to psychological development and hence to true relationship.

Although relationships form a major portion of the problems brought into analytic therapy, the Jungian literature focused on them is relatively sparse, especially in Jung's own writings. Except for two essays, "Marriage as a Psychological Relationship" and "The Love Problem of the Student" (both in volume 17 of the *Collected Works*), Jung's statements on relationship (apart from the transference in analysis) were incidental to other topics. However, some of his students, and their students, have dealt with topics which Jung did not pursue.

Among the "first generation" of Jungians, Eleanor Bertine published in 1958 a book entitled *Human Relationships: In the Family, in Friendship, in Love*. She advanced some of the topics Jung had discussed and supplemented them with chapters on the family, individual and the group, and friendship.

In a book first published in 1933, *The Way of All Women*, M. Esther Harding, another Jungian pioneer, also discussed some topics about which Jung had not written. Her focus was on the individual woman's psychology, but she included marriage and maternity as well as relationships that are "off the beaten track"—extramarital female-male relationships. In discussing friendship in some depth, she predated Bertine. She also gave some attention to female homosexuality, but not as a long-term option. In *The "I" and the "Not-I"* (1965) Harding made a further contribution to the psychology of relationship by focusing on unconscious counterparts within the family, between persons of the same sex and of opposite sexes, and the undergirdings of all these in the archetypal world.

Some increase in Jungian writing on relationship had occurred in the past two decades. Most of these works are on the relationships of heterosexual lovers: such titles as *Marriage: Dead or Alive* (Adolf Guggenbühl-Craig, 1977), *On the Way to the Wedding: Transforming the Love Relationship* (Linda Schierse Leonard, 1986), *We: Understanding the Psychology of Romantic Love* (Robert A. Johnson, 1983), *The Invisible Partners: How the Male and Female in Each of Us Affects Our Relationships* (John A. Sanford, 1980), and *Coming Together—Coming Apart: The Union of Opposites in Relationships* (John A. Desteian, 1989). Verena Kast examined mythological figures of lovers and other relationship pairs in *The Nature of Loving: Patterns of Human Relationship* (1984).

In discussions of relationships other than those of male-female lovers, Harding again led the way. Her book *The Parental Image: Its Injury and Reconstruction* (1965) considered the parent-child relationship archetypally. Sanford discussed communication as essential to relationship in *Between People: Communicating One-to-One* (1982). Liz Greene looked at various kinds of relationships through astrological glasses in *Relating: An Astrological Guide to Living* (1977). Linda Leonard discussed a matter of personal importance to every woman in *The Wounded Woman: Healing the Father-Daughter Relationship* (1982). Christine Downing's *Psyche's Sisters* (1988) takes up an area of relationship important to nearly all women; many of those without actual sisters have sisterlike friends.

Many Jungian essays and a few other books contribute to our understanding of personal relationships, but the ones I have mentioned give the flavor.

Mary Ann Mattoon

THE ROLE OF PROJECTION IN RELATIONSHIP

Crucial in the development of a relationship is projection, a major concept in Jungian thought as well as in Freudian: the expectations and assumptions—largely unconscious—that each of us has about other people. While some projections are barriers to psychological relationship, others provide a necessary introduction into an association that may lead to relationship.

The word *projection* literally means "throwing forward." The metaphor is that of a film projector, which throws onto a screen an image that has been recorded on a film in the projecting machine. Psychologically, I—as projector—perceive in another person (the screen) a content that belongs to my unconscious psyche (the film image).

Some of these contents are perceived as negative, others as positive. Negative projections are highly important in psychological development. They reveal to us the "shadow," the hidden, seemingly undesirable contents of our unconscious psyches. But they do not usually lead to relationships. We tend to see the negative qualities in other persons, whom we then avoid.

Positive projections can lead to the development of relationship. They make us want to move closer to a person in whom we perceive positive qualities. We like such a person: have warm feelings for her, are fascinated by him. We seize opportunities to spend time in the person's presence and enjoy the positive qualities we see.

After a while, we discover that the person is not so remarkable as we had thought. The positive qualities are not so marked, and there are some qualities that we find to be negative. We must revise our image and expectations of the person. A conflict may arise out of our disappointed expectations.

With conflict comes a moment of crisis for one's connection with this person. One or both of us may decide that the pain is too great, the rewards too small. Indifference may result, dislike, or even hatred—to a degree that destroys the positive connection. It is also possible, however, that each discovers the other's vulnerabilities and can accept them. Thus, projections begin to be withdrawn. Now the two people are brought together by their common humanity, and a true psychological relationship begins. There are enough positive feelings to provide the "glue," enough negative to provide challenge.

One of the first Jungian lecturers I heard described a psychological relationship as resembling two apples touching, rather than two circles overlapping. Many of the students present were shocked; the romantic notion of merging with the Other had been challenged. Only gradually could we come to realize that it takes a relatively complete person to have an open, free, and satisfying relationship with another relatively complete person. We can avoid some of the difficulties of unsatisfied expectations when we truly understand that the other person belongs to himself or herself (just as I belong to myself); then each of us can give to the other out of freedom and self-acceptance.

THE NEGATIVE SIDE OF RELATIONSHIP

Not all the negative aspects of relationship arise out of projection. Each of us has shadow qualities that are difficult, even destructive, for other persons. For example, if I am angry because of disappointed expectations, I may hurt the other person by sharp words or by creating a poisonous atmosphere. Reconciliation can occur only when I am able to own my anger and my expectations—acknowledge them as mine—and thus let go of blaming the other person. This owning is more easily said than done. My negative feelings about myself become activated, and I am likely to seek a scapegoat for such feelings. The person nearest at hand, with whom I may feel safest, is likely to get the brunt of those feelings, although he or she may have had no part in the original disappointment.

Other negative aspects of relationship have to do with the need for boundaries. The term describes the need of each of us not to be intruded upon. I must come to know my own needs and limitations, and define myself. I must not allow another person to define me.

The most destructive way in which boundaries are crossed occurs when one party forces his or her will on the other. (Some relationships, such as parent-child, include necessary and acceptable authority, but based on unequal experience, not the parent's need for power.) Such interactions are being recognized, increasingly, as *abusive*. But where there is abuse, there can be no genuine relationship. Abusive behavior destroys relationship.

PROJECTION IN VARIOUS MODELS OF RELATIONSHIP

Although projection is operative, presumably, in all human associations, it carries varying degrees of energy and "clout." Between pairs who are relatively equal—friends, coworkers, sometimes siblings—any kind of projection can go in either direction. To each person the other can be enthusiastic or sad, angry or tender, powerful or weak. Between persons of unequal status or power, some kinds of projection are more likely to be one-directional. For example, one appears to be more powerful than is actually the case, the other weaker.

The initial projection between parent and child is the

phenomenon we call bonding. The Jungian view specifies that the child sees in the parents the archetypal (i.e., generically human) mother and father, then gradually forms an individual image according to personal experience. If all goes well, by the time the son or daughter reaches adulthood, a true psychological relationship may exist with one or both parents.

Siblings usually begin their association in a condition of inequality, often based on age. Fraternal twins, with no age difference, may perceive inequality based on temperament or gender; even identical twins tend to assign more dominance to one, more submission to the other. A child is not as dependent on the sibling as on the parent but may experience both rivalry and kinship with the brother or sister. Projections between brother-sister pairs are likely to be even more complicated than those between same-sex siblings. Like parent-child projections, sibling projections may be resolved, largely, by the time the siblings reach adulthood.

TYPOLOGY IN RELATIONSHIP

The Jungian theory that is best supported empirically is that of typology, especially the attitude types, introversion and extraversion. Studies using tests of Jungian types provide some evidence.[3] More solid support can be found, however, in H. J. Eysenck's extensive work.[4] Jung's function types (thinking, feeling, intuition, sensation), while not so well established empirically, are clinically as significant as the attitude types.

The effect of differing typologies on relationships has received a great deal of popular and scientific attention. The evidence is mixed on whether polar opposites attract in the choice of marriage partners. Whether they do or

not, there is rarely complete typological consonance between two people in a relationship. Consequently, conflicts in marriage, as in other relationships, can arise out of
differing attitudes and function types. For example, one
partner, who is more introverted, may want more solitude
and interactions that are mostly one-to-one; the other,
who is more extraverted, may yearn for frequent participation in parties and other group situations.

Type-based differences are likely to occur in other ways.
For example, in spending money one person may follow
"principles" such as giving to causes, while his or her
friend or partner wants to express generosity on a more
personal level. If a common bank account, a cooperative
project, or a joint purchase is at stake, a quarrel may ensue.

The mechanism of projection is operative here, too.
When another person takes a stance different from mine, I
am likely to project inequality. I see that person as acting
on an inferior system of principles or values. Or I see the
person as purporting to be superior, and my fear of
inferiority is activated.

As is true in the face of other problems, such mutual
projections threaten the relationship. But eventually it may
be strengthened, after the two have come to understand—
at a new depth—each other's point of view.

BUILDING RELATIONSHIP

The achievement of psychological relationship is a satisfying process, but painful and never-ending. Two human
beings find a way to take into account the assets, needs,
complexities, and limitations of each. They share joy,
pain, and insights and listen intently to each other. Each
works to articulate inner experiences as well as responses
to the other person and the world around both of them.

Each acknowledges feeling hurt and guilty as well as nourished and uplifted. Conflicts must be suffered until deeper understanding of oneself and the other results.

In "unequal" relationships the process is modified. For example, teacher and student must make allowances for the irreducible inequality of experience and power. Similarly, the parent listens to the child's emotional responses to all aspects of life, while the parent tells the child only what affects both of them. The parent must continue to nurture even while working out a dispute with the child.

Between lovers the relationship probably suffers the least limitations. Sharing can occur on all levels, including the sexual. But the sharing is not consistently satisfactory. Hence, myriad conflicts can arise. The process of resolving conflict, however, can lead to greater depth and intimacy in the relationship.

Between friends, equality of status gives the relationship maximum possibilities, excluding the sexual. (If the friends become sexual partners, the relationship may evolve into one of lovers, or there may be a complicated movement between the realms of friendship and erotic love.) Unlike members of a family, however, friends are free to walk away from each other. Hence, there is great need for prompt and thorough resolution of differences.

None of these developments can occur, of course, unless there are deep satisfactions for both parties in the relationship, to make the difficult times worthwhile. To stay in an association that is totally negative suggests pathology. Indeed, it is hard to imagine consciousness in a completely negative association.

THE ROLE OF RELATIONSHIP IN INDIVIDUATION

Individuation is Jung's concept of the process by which a person becomes more nearly whole, that is, undivided.

The process also makes one unique, differentiated from other persons.

Relationship contributes to individuation through the projecting of unconscious contents onto another person and, eventually, the withdrawal of such projections. Thus the relationship gives me the possibility of integrating unconscious—shadow—contents into consciousness. For example, I may have looked to my friend or partner for encouragement to deal with the world of money management. As I face my fears, accept responsibility, and learn about money matters, I enlarge my consciousness and become more nearly whole.

Individuation is not the same as happiness and well-being. Indeed, as Adolf Guggenbühl-Craig pointed out in his book *Marriage: Dead or Alive,* the goal of marriage is not happiness but rather individuation. Happiness may depend on the spouse's living up to one's expectations; individuation depends on developing in oneself the capacities one has expected and perhaps enjoyed in the spouse. A person does not give up such expectations without pain.

Many clients enter therapy because of problems that are manifested in relationships or the lack thereof. It is important in Jungian therapy that the therapist and client not focus primarily on solving the problem. Rather, the client needs help in experiencing that life problem—like others— as a stimulus to psychological development and, ultimately, to the individuation process.

Much of our life energy goes into association with other humans. These associations parallel our development: from dependent child to adult, with peer relationships in each era of life. We can continue to project maturity and strength onto other people, or we can undergo the suffering that comes from taking responsibility for our own lives. With effort, connection to the unconscious psyche, and the help of friends and perhaps therapists, our associations become transformed into relationships. In the process of this transformation and the further development of relationships, they can contribute immeasurably to our psychological development and, ultimately, to our wholeness.

NOTES

1. C. G. Jung, CW, 10, para. 326.
2. Ibid., para. 579.
3. See, e.g., D. Cook, "Is Jung's Typology True?," *Dissertation Abstracts International* (1971), 31, 2979B–2980B.
4. See, e.g., H. J. Eysenck, *Dimensions of Personality* (London: Kegan Paul, Trench, Trubner, 1947).

Part Three

AMONG
PROFESSIONALS

The Management of Closeness in Jungian Training Societies

An Organizational Analysis

Karl E. Weick

To scholars of organizational theory, the organizational forms found in learned societies dedicated to training have unusual properties. Among these is the fact that much of the organization exists only in the mind and is repeatedly rebuilt, through contentious interaction, out of images based on incomplete learning cycles. When organizations form around the combination of clinical training activities, complex theories of change, autonomous professionals, and charismatic leaders, they tend to cohere only so long as members are able to sustain the belief that there is shared agreement about what ends are important and what means are appropriate to reach them. As these tacit agreements begin to unravel, training activities tend to be conducted with greater variation than anyone intended, and the quality of the training experience and the trainees becomes more variable.

The purpose of this chapter is to explore how organizational dynamics such as these determine the effectiveness of training societies. I shall discuss a Jungian training society as the prototype for issues that arise in training societies in general. The argument will be developed in the following way. First, I look at four characteristics of Jungian training society members that affect the kinds of organizations they create. These four characteristics include suspicion of organizations, predisposition to introverted intuitive planning, reluctance to act their way into new meanings, and changing views of appropriate means and ends. Second, I look at three properties of the training society itself including its size, its dispersion, and the difficulty of its self-imposed task. Third, I argue that these several dynamics interact to complicate boundary issues between supervising therapists and candidates, and can lead to a higher incidence of problematic liaisons. In the fourth and final section, I review the few sources of organization that exist in training societies and argue that special efforts must be made to preserve them.

MEMBERS OF TRAINING SOCIETIES

Suspicion of Organizations

The phrase "Jungian training society" is close to an oxymoron, judging from Jung's aversion to large organizations. This aversion is not lost on members of the society and should pervade its culture and weaken collective controls.

Joseph Wheelwright's conversation with Jung in 1951 is representative:

> "You know, Dr. Jung, I did it!"
> "Really? What is it you did?"
> "That training center we were talking about in 1939. Well, we had a lot of help, of course, but it's going, it's going! We have lots of candidates—two—and we have five card-bearing members; it's really . . ."
> Then I saw he had a faraway look, as though he'd

moved off, and I said, "Well, I can see you're not very fascinated."

"No, to tell you the truth, I am not very fascinated. There's really nothing I would less rather talk about." (Up to then I had been full of enthusiasm, but this did dampen me a bit.) "Well, that isn't very nice of me. I see you're quite upset, and I suppose you must have some sort of an organization. Why don't you try to have the most disorganized organization you can manage?"

"Oh, we have, Dr. Jung! We have!"[1]

As Jung said in a different setting, "The heaping together of paintings by Old Masters in museums is a catastrophe; likewise a collection of a hundred Great Brains makes on big fathead."[2]

People who are suspicious of most attempts at organization often fail to differentiate between those that are helpful and those that are stifling. The kind of organization most people fear is one that is built either of first-order controls such as direct orders, surveillance, and rules and regulations, or second-order controls such as standardization and specialization.[3] Fears are focused on these organizational forms because they are the most conspicuous and most overtly controlling.

But people often forget that there is a third source of control, namely, common assumptions and premises that direct attention to specific events and evoke specific behaviors. Third-order controls are important sources of organization when problems are nonroutine, blanket rules are inapplicable, outputs are not standardized, and raw materials come in all shapes and sizes.

Organizations built from third-order controls allow for greater discretionary action, which is important when the beliefs that people share consist of complex theories with diverse implications. Third-order controls are more appropriate when recruitment and socialization are based on identification with the society and internalization of its values, than when recruitment is based simply on compliance to gain the rewards that the society controls.[4]

People who are suspicious of organizations tend to avoid visible trappings of first- and second-order control such as rules, regulations, and specialties, but in doing so, they tend also to overlook the degree to which agreements, common beliefs, and shared interpretations are all that remain to bind people together. Thus, they tend to treat disagreements as a nuisance and fail to realize that by doing so they have put the organization in jeopardy. When third-order controls are neglected, both control and effectiveness decrease, and the incidence of problems increases.

The Predominance of Introverted Intuitives

Jungian training societies appear to have a skewed distribution of personality types, which compounds some of their organizational problems. Jungians are predominantly introverted intuitives (Jung himself was an introverted intuitive thinking type), whereas Freudians tend to be extroverted sensation types.[5] Wheelwright, the champion of the training society, and himself an extraverted intuitive feeling type, stated frankly, "had it not been for the S [sensation] types the Jung Institute would have folded."[6] So the types best able to save the institute tend to be the types that are most scarce within it.

But the organizational issue here is even more fascinating. Edward F. Edinger describes a person with the introverted attitude this way: "functions most satisfactorily on his own and when free from pressure to adapt to the external . . . prefers his own company and is reserved or uncomfortable in large groups."[7] Jung's description is similar:

> He holds aloof from external happenings, does not join in, has a distinct dislike of society as soon as he finds himself among too many people. In a large gathering he feels lonely and lost. The more crowded it is, the greater becomes his resistance. He is not in the least "with it," and has no love of enthusiastic get-togethers. He is not a good mixer. What he does, he does in his own way, barricading himself against influences from the outside.[8]

Thus it is not surprising that introverts would be suspicious of groups, wary of their controls, and casual about processes that hold people together. And it is hard to imagine a better way to realize Jung's dream of a disorganized organization than to tell two hundred introverts to get organized.

Intuitives tend to be driven more by intentions, plans, and possibilities than by close attention to what is actually happening. That's partly why the sensation types were the only ones who could save the institute. The complication for organizational functioning in having a preponderance of planners is that when people plan to do something, the plan is often treated as if the thing has already been done. This happens all the time in organizations where plans are symbols,[9] "in the sense that when an organization does not know how it is doing or knows that it is failing, it can signal a different message to observers. If the organization does not have a compact car in its line, it can announce plans to have one. On the basis of this announcement the firm may be valued more highly than an organization that makes no such announcement. It is less crucial that the organization is actually planning to make the car than that all concerned imagine this to be the case."[10]

An organization of intuitives is an organization that is susceptible to mistaking its intentions for its accomplishments. If intuitives "read" their environment in terms of possibilities, they may easily overlook some immediate issues that are tangible threats, giving thought privilege over action.

Introverted, intuitive thinkers are verbal, inwardly focused people concerned with possibilities. Against this backdrop, it is tempting to privilege thought and to assume that people think their way into the meanings, strategies, interventions, policies, and actions they eventually display.

Much organizational life is not organized this way, nor does it have its origins in thought. Because organizations are programmed to generate action[11] and are characterized by routines for doing so,[12] their rationality often takes the form of retrospective justification of elapsed action rather than prospective deliberation of future action. Organizations more often find themselves bound to prior actions that must be explained than to prior beliefs that must be enacted. Thus organizations tend to act their way into meanings and what they do constrains what they know.

Obviously not all actions need to be explained. Research with behavioral commitment suggests that when people take action that is visible, irrevocable, and volitional, they become bound to these actions and feel compelled to justify them.[13] Furthermore, one of the few ways they become freed from these actions and their justifications is to perceive that anyone in the same position would have done the same thing. The perception that they were "forced" to act reduces volition, weakens commitment, and makes the justification less resistant to change.

This discussion of action is background to the observation that training societies are ideal sites that bind people to actions and encourage justification. Actions are made public through meetings and newsletters; participation in self-initiated projects is voluntary; and actions become difficult to reverse when they are preserved in case notes, witnessed by supervisors, and discussed among candidates. Training societies, especially Jungian societies, are good contexts to generate justifications because members are verbal people who admire a charismatic theorist whose life is well documented for purposes of modeling, whose rationale for everything is spelled out, and yet who retained sufficient ambiguity in what he wrote, said, and lived, that those traces can be interpreted differently.

The importance of these observations is that training societies may find themselves espousing with passion an odd mixture of beliefs and assumptions for reasons that are not altogether clear to them. Furthermore, when they try to change these beliefs, nothing happens. Thus, the organization is stuck with outdated beliefs that prove to be surprisingly resistant to change. One clue as to what may be going on here is that the beliefs were formed as justifications for individual actions in early stages of the society. The justifications persist, become adopted by other people, and form part of the culture. The justifications are resistant because none of the appeals for change address the issues of volition, visibility, and irrevocability that bound people to the actions in the first place.

Thus, training societies are blunt instruments, not only because members are more concerned with possibilities than with the present, but also because their interpretations often are colored by justifications that grew up around actions that occurred much earlier to a different set of issues. Despite their inappropriateness, these dated justifications persist because few people realize that they defend prior actions for which the proponent felt responsible. People preoccupied with symbols rather than actions tend to underestimate the role of action in the persistence of meaning.

Disagreements in Organizations
People in training societies are professionals who deal with nonroutine problems using underdeveloped paradigms. These conditions create ambiguity, conflict, and disagreement, which has implications for the kind of organizational structure and strategy that will be effective.[14] Consideration of this point links our concern with members to our concern with properties of organization, which we pursue in the next section.

James Thompson and Arthur Tuden[15] made the influential proposal that patterns of agreement and disagreement on means and ends dictate what will be the most appropriate strategy to make decisions. Agreement on both means and ends favors a computation strategy such as one finds in a pure bureaucracy. If people agree on means but not on ends, the preferred strategy is compromise among representatives such as one might find in the UN Security Council. If people agree on ends but not on means, this leads to the decision strategy of judgment where the entire membership pools its evidence and then votes, as in a board of directors. When people agree on neither means nor ends, organizational politics intensify,[16] and the only recourse is "inspiration" from such diverse sources as charismatic leaders or cults.

This view of patterns of agreement and their implications for organizations implies that training societies will be effective if they either choose decision strategies that fit their current pattern of agreement or change their disagreements to fit the decision strategy they already have in place. Either approach should lead to fewer training problems than would treating the issues of decision strategy structure and disagreements as unrelated.

ORGANIZATIONAL PROPERTIES

Organizational Size
Training organizations tend to be large and growing larger, which means that issues of distance, closeness, and, in Jung's case, morals come into play. Jung's views on size were quite explicit and undoubtedly have an effect on people who administer the society. Here are three examples of those views:

1. "The morality of society as a whole is in inverse ratio to its size."[17]
2. "Hence, every man is, in a certain sense, unconsciously a worse man when he is in society than when acting alone; for he is carried by society and to that extent relieved of his individual responsibility."[18]
3. "Any large company composed of wholly admirable persons has the morality and intelligence of an unwieldy, stupid, and violent animal. The bigger the organization, the more unavoidable is its immorality and blind stupidity. . . . Society, by automatically stressing all the collective qualities in its individual representatives, puts a premium on mediocrity, on everything that settles down to vegetate in an easy, irresponsible way. Individuality will inevitably be driven to the wall. . . . In a small social body, the individuality of its members is better safeguarded; and the greater is their relative freedom and the

possibility of conscious responsibility. Without freedom, there can be no morality."[19]

Strong stuff! If collectives are this immoral and unregulated, then it should come as no surprise that large training societies have sticky problems and are only moderately effective. As with other organizational variables, however, the issue of size is complicated.

Consistent with Jung's statements, increased size can lead to decreased morality through several routes. In large groups, people feel more anonymous, responsibility becomes diffused more widely, and restraints are thereby weakened. In large groups, persuasive appeals must reach the lowest common denominator, or as Georg Simmel put it, "what is common to all can be the property of only those who possess least."[20] The beliefs that diffuse widely are those that tend to be older, simpler, more absolute, more primitive, more extreme, and less differentiated. And, as groups get larger, there is also a better chance that individuals will find a handful of people who are just like them, which means they receive support and validation for whatever position they take.

Despite these effects of increasing size, none of them, in Jung's words, "crush individuals morally and spiritually."[21] For example, size also tends to be positively correlated with ambiguity, which means that individuals are more likely to respond on a dispositional rather than situational basis. As Lazarus and Folkman show, "whenever there is ambiguity, personal factors shape the understanding of the situation, thereby making the interpretation of the situation more a function of the person than of objective stimulus constraints."[22] With increased size, psychological types should be more influential and should exert more control over the substance of the organization.

Thus, increased size need not blot out freedom, individuality, or morality.

In fact, size can facilitate the establishment of identity. When people join a small specialized group, their individuality is expressed by the membership and does not tend to develop separately. As the group gets larger and its identity becomes more diffuse, individuals tend to develop an identity apart from the group. The elements of a distinctive circle are undifferentiated; the elements of an undistinctive circle are differentiated.[23]

Regardless of whether people become individuals in small or large groups—and I'm trying to make the case that differentiation can occur in both settings—it remains true that when differentiation and individuality increase, that is no guarantee of virtue. "All the highest achievements of virtue as well as the blackest villainies, are individual."[24] So an increase in "individual responsibility" will often lead to more extreme responses, but those responses are not necessarily more moral.

The Dispersed Nature of the Organization
Training societies tend to be spread out over a large area with loose connections between people. This configuration creates unique problems that place even a greater premium on shared images.

An example of a problem related to dispersion is the venerable distinction between centralization and decentralization. One paraphrase of Jung's fondness for disorganized organizations is that he had a strong preference for decentralized organizational forms that allowed for local interpretation and decision making to deal with nonroutine problems.

There is an interesting subtlety in the success of decentralized forms, which Phillip Selznick spotted.[25] Whenever you find a successful decentralized organization, if you look at what happened just before the successful period of decentralization, you usually find that the organization went through an intense period of centralization. During the period of centralization, premises and assumptions became more homogenous so that, once people decentralized, they thought about issues similarly and fewer overt controls were necessary. When organizations move from centralization to decentralization, this often corresponds to a move from heterogeneous values, assumptions, and premises, to more homogeneous positions on a handful of key issues.

What is interesting about many training societies is that they seem to be decentralized organizations with heterogeneous values. Thus they have neither centralization nor homogeneity to hold them together and must rely on strategies of "inspiration" or improvisation to realize their aspirations.

The Impossible Task

The impossible task that training societies have set for themselves is evident in this comment by Joseph Wheelwright:

> There is something that strikes me as awfully difficult and troublesome about the custom [in Jungian training centers] of casting the training analyst in the simultaneous roles of judge and therapist. To my mind these two roles are mutually exclusive, and this practice bothers me a great deal. If I could have my way about this, the training analyst would actually be disqualified from having anything to do with the promotion of the candidate.[26]

To be therapist and judge is exceedingly difficult. To see this, think of the training relationship as a setting of inequality. The goal in such a relationship is to make the inequality temporary and to move to equality. This is difficult because such relationships are often designed to serve the needs of the dominant party, and the lesser person is often more concerned with "being a good lesser" rather than making the change from lesser to full stature. It is hard for the dominant person to know how many rights to grant the lesser. Furthermore, it is hard for the dominant person to maintain perception of the lesser "as a person of as much intrinsic worth as the superior."[27]

If we view the relationship of temporary inequality from the subordinate's point of view, three things become apparent. First, subordinates concentrate on survival, which means that direct, honest, sincere actions in one's own self-interest are muted. Instead, disguised and indirect ways of acting are used to accommodate and please the dominant group. Second, subordinates know more about the dominants than the dominants know about the subordinates. They have to if they are to survive. And third, subordinates know more about dominants than themselves. There is little purpose in knowing oneself if knowledge of the dominants determines one's life. All three dynamics stylize interaction, which restricts realistic evaluation. And all three suggest that, in the eyes of the candidate, the judge displaces the therapist, which confirms Wheelwright's worst fears.

The dominant therapist-judge also suffers in such a system. This person gets little information concerning his or her impact on candidates, so change appears to be unnecessary. Even if the therapist has a vague sense that something is wrong, feedback will be too blurred to be of much value as a guide.

The point of these considerations is that even if training societies were conventional hierarchical organizations with all three types of control systems, they would still be ineffective so long as the tasks of judge and therapist were combined in the same person. When this task is performed in an organization that is underspecified, underorganized, loosely coupled, and maintained largely through diverse images held in the minds of its members, the chances of it being accomplished effectively are reduced even more. The temporary inequality becomes more permanent and more open to exploitation, as we will see.

PROBLEMATIC LIAISONS IN TRAINING RELATIONSHIPS

We have already seen that the relationship of analyst to candidate is one of temporary inequality embedded in an organization with diffuse third-order controls. To understand more about problematic liaisons,[28] we need to see that on top of this temporary inequality is often imposed the more permanent inequality of male-female relationships.

The distribution of power in these relationships is reflected by the observation that women usually build relationships in settings where subordination is part of the definition. "The condition of being a man is not defined as subordinate to women by force. Looking at the facts of the abuses of women all at once, you see that a woman is socially defined as a person who, whether or not she is or has been, can be treated in these ways by men at any time, and little, if anything, will be done about it. This is what it means when feminists say that maleness is a form of power and femaleness is a form of powerlessness."[29]

Power differentials affect epistemology. They influence

who is able to say what is real and have that definition accepted. It is in this context that one can understand the feminists' insistence that people should not mistake silence for absence. The unnamed should not be mistaken for the nonexistent.

> The world is not entirely the way the powerful say it is or want to believe it is. If it appears to be, it is because power constructs the appearance of reality by silencing the voices of the powerless, by excluding them from access to authoritative discourse. Powerlessness means that when you say, "This is how it is," it is *not* taken as being that way. This makes articulating silence, perceiving the presence of absence, believing those who have been stripped of credibility, critically contextualizing what passes for simple fact, necessary.[30]

If we focus these considerations on issues of domination and submission in training relationships, it becomes clearer that inequalities, both permanent and temporary, mold people's perceptions of what they are doing when they train. Interventions often seem geared more toward preserving inequality than toward moving the relationship from one of inequality to equality.

Take the specific issue of the "unwanted imposition of sexual requirements in the context of a relationship of unequal power."[31] Training is about development, growth, and differentiation in a context of trust. Sexuality is part of that development. "Most women wish to choose whether, when, where, and with whom to have sexual relationships, as one important part of exercising control over their lives. Sexual harassment denies this choice,"[32] and in denying it, substitutes pressure and sexual exactions for growth and insight. What people want is "sexual connection undominated by dominance, unimplicated in the inequality of the sexes, a sexuality of one's own yet with another, both of whom are equally present because yes is meaningful because no is meaningful."[33]

The training relationship is compounded of three inequalities, one sexual (powerful males and powerless females), one economic (if you're not certified, you can't accept clients as a Jungian analyst and charge accordingly), and one structural (teacher and student). That relationship is vulnerable to exploitation, especially considering the type of organization within which it occurs.

To protect the training relationship, members of training societies must reaffirm individually and collectively that this relationship is based on trust built out of honesty, sincerity, and loyalty.[34] If those three building blocks are lost, then trust also disappears, and all that is left is raw power.

Even though a context of trust is crucial, it is tough to "enforce" it in an organization where people pride themselves on their professionalism, autonomy, and discretion; where authority, formalization, and centralization are suspect; and where most of the important business occurs behind closed doors. Since enforcement won't work, people have to resort to shared images and symbols if they want to hold the organization together and produce the effective training it was intended to administer.

To use symbols and images more deliberately means that people have to become more self-conscious of the ways in which commitments, organizational culture, norms, identification, and social constructions work to organize people's actions, even when they are not face to face. If members allow their images of what they stand for to get blurred; if they fail to monitor, reaffirm, and update them; if they neglect to use them when they interpret what people are doing; if they fail to use them when they talk to others on behalf of the society; if they tolerate all of these lapses in what the organization is; and if they forget that people must continually rebuild this kind of organization, then members will trigger pathologies even they will find surprising.

Training societies such as those established by Jungians are held together by third-order controls, controls that are as much in members' heads as they are on paper or in manuals of procedure. These third-order controls are invisible, easy to neglect, easy to take for granted, easy to alter inadvertently. The reason they get so little attention is that they don't look like organization in the same way such things as formal rules and published routines look like organization. Conventional trappings such as rules and routines do have a place in organizations. But they assume a secondary position when the large, dispersed organization consists of professionals defined by expertise and values, nonroutine problems, and people who disagree about means and ends. Faced with this context, when people try to manage what is perhaps the most complex social form there is—that of being simultaneously therapist and judge in a training relationship—it is not surprising that such a difficult relationship is handled in idiosyncratic ways that sometimes undercut educational objectives.

When Jung told Wheelwright to build the most disorganized organization he could manage, Jung did not say do away with organization altogether. And training societies have not. But they have reduced organization to a point where everyone bears responsibility for what remains.

The minimal organization that still exists in training societies seems to consist of shared affirmations, restrictions, and permissions that define what is appropriate and inappropriate. This normative order can be unstable unless people have intense feelings of approval and disapproval regarding appropriate behavior and consensus about what constitutes appropriate behavior. If both of these conditions are met, then therapists and candidates are more likely to perceive that a social control system is in place. They perceive that someone who knows and cares is paying close attention to what is being done and can tell when deviations from expectations are occurring.[35] This perception becomes consequential when people realize that, to be accepted in the society, they need to live up to these expectations.

The problem with this form of control system is that it cannot be imposed by the leaders at the top. Top-down control works for systems tied together by first- and second-order controls, but that's not the type of system found in training societies. Instead, social control systems emerge from interactions in which members negotiate meanings, share symbols, and build commitments. To manage a system of this kind means to increase the occasions for interaction, explicitly address the question of the discrepancy between a current and a desired normative order, identify expectations about which people feel strongly and on which they can agree, and then commit them to this order. The "feedstock" for this entire process is candid information sharing, extensive interaction, recognition of the high stakes involved (for instance, possible litigation, survival of the society, credibility, perpetuation of an important body of theory and practice), and a psychologically safe environment in which to change.[36]

An organization of third-order controls would please Jung because it is a disorganized organization that remains manageable. It is disorganized because members have diverse beliefs and expectations on most issues that are discussed in the society. On a handful of issues judged central to effectiveness, however, their beliefs are more convergent and this creates the organization amidst disorganization. The tricky part in managing a system like this is to negotiate what is central and what is peripheral. The preceding analysis suggests that the issue of what is central and peripheral in the normative order that holds the training society together has been treated too casually. In a third-order control system, organizations do not simply *have* shared beliefs, they *are* their shared beliefs. Shared beliefs are synonymous with organization and the only glue that holds the system together and gives it an identity. To treat those beliefs as incidental byproducts of an organization, rather than its essence, is to strip away any meaningful context that could limit exploitation.

The intellectual and analytical power of Jungian analysts comes in large part from their understanding of the fundamental ways in which symbols animate, organize, and summarize diverse experience. All I'm urging is that Jungians should apply that same sensitivity and understanding to the problems that beset their own training societies. In a profound sense, a training society is a creature of symbols with which people invest it and how those symbols are managed.

NOTES

I am indebted to Dr. Harry Wilmer for his help in thinking through these ideas.

1. Joseph B. Wheelwright, *St. George and the Dandelion: Forty Years of Practice as a Jungian Analyst* (San Francisco: C. G. Jung Institute of San Francisco, 1982), p. 59.
2. C. G. Jung, *Psychological Reflections* (Princeton, N.J.: Princeton University Press, 1973), p. 166.

3. Charles Perrow, "The Bureaucratic Paradox: The Efficient Organization Centralizes in Order to Decentralize," in *Organizational Dynamics* 5, no. 4 (1977): 3–14.

4. Herbert C. Kelman, "Compliance, Identification, and Internalization: Three Processes of Attitude Change," in *Journal of Conflict Resolution* 2 (1958): 51–60.

5. Wheelwright, *St. George and the Dandelion*, p. 57.

6. Ibid., p. 76.

7. Edward F. Edinger, "An Outline of Analytical Psychology," in *Quadrant* (1968), p. 2.

8. Jung, *Psychological Types, Collected Works* 6 (Princeton, N.J.: Princeton University Press, 1976), p. 550.

9. Michael D. Cohen and James G. March, *Leadership and Ambiguity* (New York: McGraw-Hill), 1974.

10. Karl E. Weick, *The Social Psychology of Organizing* (Reading, Mass.: Addison-Wesley, 1979), p. 10.

11. William H. Starbuck, "Organizations as Action Generators," in *American Sociological Review* 48 (1983): 91–102.

12. Martha S. Feldman, *Order without Design* (Stanford, Calif.: Stanford University Press, 1989).

13. Gerald R. Salancik, "Commitment and the Control of Organizational Behavior and Belief," in Barry M. Staw and Gerald R. Salancik, eds., *New Directions in Organizational Behavior* (Chicago: St. Clair, 1977), pp. 1–54. Charles A. O'Reilly and David F. Caldwell, "The Commitment and Job Tenure of New Employees: Some Evidence of Postdecisional Justification," in *Administrative Science Quarterly* 26 (1981): 597–616.

14. Karl E. Weick and Reuben McDaniel, "How Professional Organizations Work: Implications for School Organization and Management," in Thomas Sergiovanni, ed., *Schooling for Tomorrow* (Rockleigh, N.J.: Allyn and Bacon, 1989), pp. 330–355.

15. James D. Thompson and Arthur Tuden, "Strategies, Structures and Process of Organizational Decision Making," in J. D. Thompson, P. W. Hawkes, B. H. Junker, and A.

Tuden, eds., *Comparative Studies in Administration* (Pittsburgh: University of Pittsburgh Press, 1959), pp. 195–216.

16. Jeffrey Pfeffer, *Power in Organizations* (Marshfield, Mass.: Pitman, 1981), p. 71.

17. Jung, *Psychological Reflections* (Princeton, N.J.: Princeton University Press, 1973), p. 165.

18. Ibid., p. 165.

19. Ibid., p. 166.

20. Georg Simmel, *The Sociology of Georg Simmel* (New York: Free Press, 1950), p. 37.

21. Jung, *Psychological Reflections,* p. 165.

22. Richard S. Lazarus and Susan Folkman, *Stress, Appraisal, and Coping* (New York: Springer, 1984), p. 104.

23. G. Simmel, "Group Expansion and the Development of Individuality," in G. Simmel, *On Individuality and Social Forms* (Chicago: University of Chicago Press, 1971), pp. 251–293.

24. Jung, *Psychological Reflections,* p. 165.

25. Phillip G. Selznick, *Leadership in Administration* (New York: Harper and Row, 1957), pp. 112–119.

26. Wheelwright, *St. George and the Dandelion,* p. 34.

27. Jean Baker Miller, *Towards a New Psychology of Women* (Boston: Beacon Press, 1976), p. 5.

28. Glen O. Gabbard, ed., *Sexual Exploitation in Professional Relationships* (Washington: American Psychiatric Press, 1989).

29. Catharine A. MacKinnon, *Feminism Unmodified: Discourses on Life and Law* (Cambridge, Mass.: Harvard University Press, 1987), pp. 170–171.

30. Ibid., p. 164.

31. Catherine A. MacKinnon, *Sexual Harassment of Working Women* (New Haven: Yale University Press, 1979), p. 1.

32. Ibid., p. 25.

33. MacKinnon, *Feminism Unmodified,* p. 217.

34. Jonathan B. King, "Prisoner's Paradoxes," in *Journal of Business Ethics* 7 (1988): 475–487.

35. Charles O'Reilly, "Corporations, Culture, and Commitment," in *California Management Review* 31, no. 4 (1989): 9–25.

36. Edgar H. Schein, *Process Consultation,* vol. 2 (Reading, Mass.: Addison-Wesley, 1987), pp. 97–99.

The Candidate

James Shultz

A friend proposes, "Let's go for a boat ride next Saturday."

"I'd like to, but I'm going to a seminar."

"What for?"

"Well, it's required. You see, I'm in training to be a Jungian analyst."

"A union analyst?" He looks perplexed.

"No, a *Jungian* analyst, following C. G. Jung, as opposed to, or I should say, as distinguished from Sigmund Freud."

"Oh," he says. "How long will that take?"

"I don't really know. The shortest time in which I've heard of anyone finishing is four years. Most people take longer, and some have been in the program ten or twelve years."

"Sounds like a lot of work. I guess you'll have more patients when you're through."

"No, my practice is already full."

"You'll raise your fees, then."

"No, I'm already charging the going rate for my discipline."

"Then why *are* you doing this?"

I tell him that I expect the training to help me work with my patients, and that I think it already has. I try to describe an inner sense of being on my own life's path that is hard to put into words.

His look says he doesn't understand and maybe thinks I'm a little crazy but he accepts me anyway. "I'm sorry you can't go. Some other time."

I might be a little crazy. Maybe it helps in this business. I've been a trainee in the Inter-Regional Society of Jungian Analysts for five years and a candidate for four. The first year was "preliminary." Those are my qualifications.

Perhaps I will begin by reminding you of what a candidate is. The word comes from the Latin *candidatus*, meaning "clothed in white," and originally referred to the white toga worn by candidates for office in ancient Rome. The *Webster's* definition of "candidate" is "one presented . . . as suitable for and aspiring to an office, position, membership, right, or honor," or "one that is likely or worthy to gain a post, position, or distinction or to come to a certain place, end, or fate." Common usage in the Inter-Regional Society refers to all trainees as "candidates," although technically speaking the training period is divided into preliminary candidacy, and control stages. In this chapter, I will use "candidate" to mean all of us in the analytic training program of the Society.

When I think about closeness, I start to think about distance. Accordingly, for two or more things to be close, there has to be some distance, however small, between them. That goes whether we're talking about physical objects in proximity or people in intimate relationship with each other. With the total loss of distance we come upon union or assimilation or fusion or identification or symbiosis or *participation mystique*, some kind of mixing of the two or more that interrupts their individual integrity and changes the equation. I'm not saying that's good or bad, just that it's something other than closeness.

Being a candidate to become a Jungian analyst brings up the subject of closeness in a number of ways. In general it is as if there is a circle of people, the analysts, and in the center of that circle is the spirit of C. G. Jung. It is a little circle because there are not very many Jungian analysts—about eleven hundred in the entire world. They may not all like each other or associate with each other, but they are all connected by their common experience and title and by their "proximity" to Jung. Outside of the circle of analysts is another circle, this thin one formed by candidates, whose raison d'être is to join the inner little circle by becoming an analyst, to "get in." In this dimension, everyone else belongs on the periphery, in a third wide circle, the "outer world," if you will. In a sense, being a candidate takes one away from everyday life, causing a separation from friends and family and ordinary things such as working for a living and playing. Being a candidate creates distance. And when you are a candidate, it's clear there's a good distance between you and the analyst group as well—they make sure of that. In the "circle in between," you are as close to being an analyst as one can be without being one, yet sometimes it seems so far away you can't see how you'll ever get there. And maybe you won't. Some don't.

With regard to determining whether and when one gets to be an analyst, the analysts hold all the votes, a fact often translated into the view that the analysts hold all the power. This perspective establishes a hierarchy defined by the dominant group, the analyst members of the Society, and a nondominant or subordinate group, the candidates, who wish to be members. In light of this power differential and the binding of the candidates in it by the fact that there is no other way to become a Jungian analyst once we've chosen this one, we develop a tendency to feel and act like children vis-à-vis the analyst-parents, in a more or less natural psychological re-creation of the dynamics of the family of origin. As you might imagine, all sorts of problems have arisen from the unconscious enactment of this archetypal paradigm by candidates and analysts. (See the chapter by Karl Weick for discussion of the group dynamics and the chapter by Joseph Wakefield for a description and analysis of the interactions between candidate and analyst-supervisor)

Now I would like to enumerate some of the events of candidacy that have brought meaning to the dimension of closeness and distance for me. I offer my personal experiences to provide examples of experiences common to most candidates in our program, and perhaps to others as well.

GETTING IN: *Jumping Through the Ring of Fire*

The process of getting into training in this institute has three stages, also thought of as three hoops. First is the application itself; second and third are interviews at the regional and interregional levels. I will only comment on the third and final stage, the interregional interview.

I had never been to Birmingham. I had never had a reason to go there until I was invited to meet with the admissions committee. Six or seven of us applicants were gathered in a room with two candidates (the first ones I'd ever met) who were there to help us with our fears beforehand and whatever came up after the interviews. It's not for nothing that this room is called the "recovery room." At the appointed hour, each of us was to arrive outside the designated room (one of the analysts' hotel bedrooms) and wait to be called. If you've never stood and waited for several minutes in a hotel hallway, don't bother. It's an experience worth missing.

Two separate hour-long interviews were held in two of those rooms with five or six analysts apiece, and they all had questions. Penetrating questions. They didn't indicate how you were doing, either. They just let you know when they were through with you. Back in the recovery room, all the applicants waited for the call, when the combined interview groups (the entire admissions committee) would summon us alphabetically to receive their verdict: acceptance into training, rejection, or more interviewing until they could make up their collective mind to say "come in" or "go away, at least for now." We returned one by one, with our news and quiet joy, grief, shock, relief, grim denial, exuberance, anger, congratulations, confusion, condolences, and many tears.

We'd all been applicants together, if just for the day, and now we were split. I didn't know why I was let in and others were not, but I had my joy and they had their pain, and I wanted to get away so I wouldn't have to see them. In front of them, I was reluctant to celebrate, afraid of provoking their envy, and perhaps ashamed of a secret urge to gloat. Most of them went home, but a few stayed around for the three-day conference that followed the interviews. They could go to the academic presentations but not to the candidates' meetings. I avoided them.

Those of us who got into training together are a "class." Some didn't stay for the conference, and since we're scattered geographically, we didn't meet until the next conference a year later. But we keep up with each other if only to compare our progress, and there's a camaraderie among us. We came "through the fire" one by one together.

Two things I remember most about "getting in." One of the candidate "helpers" in the recovery room took me for a walk between interviews and helped to calm my nerves. He felt I would be accepted and told me so. Only later did I find out that the candidate representatives in these recovery rooms are usually accurate in predicting who among the applicants will make it in and who will be rejected. This friendly rep said he wanted someone to share a room with him for the conference; I volunteered, and to my surprise and delight he accepted my offer without hesitation. I felt welcomed by him first, later by others. He and I have become friends over the past four years. Now he is "gone." He graduated last spring and became an analyst. I miss him. Our friendship holds, but it is different now, with a concern about the relationship that wasn't there before. He is in that circle from which I am excluded. It makes me want to hurry up and finish my own work.

The other thing I remember most is the way I felt after those interviews. Beyond happiness and relief was the profound sense of having been opened up, "from stem to sternum," and seen all the way inside to the middle of me and left exposed. The best way I can think to describe it is that it was as if I had undergone a psychic laparotomy. They must have found no malignancy, I reasoned, or they wouldn't have let me "through the gate." But for the next two days, I awoke sobbing, with all my life's sequestered feeling right there before me. Of course I covered up to get through the day. Then, at an evening cocktail party, one of the analysts who had interviewed me at both regional and interregional levels came up from behind and, playing the trickster, said into my ear, "You fooled 'em." That shocked me and helped me close back up.

THE CANDIDATES' GROUP: *Siblings*

Another shocking event was my first "candidate meeting." I was so happy and enthusiastic and innocent, eager to meet my new colleagues and hopeful that they would like me. Then the grumbling started. The society was said to be in a crisis. The analysts were reported to be fighting among themselves, and the candidates were being ignored or victimized and had little or no recourse. Training was irregular at best. Candidates had dropped out and no one quite knew why. Some had failed exams after years of effort and had given up or been asked to leave. Confusion. And I had worked hard to get here.

It took about two years and many encounters with fellow candidates for me to feel a part of this group and to understand the general complaint. A divisive power struggle was going on in the Society, and while few of the candidates were taking sides, many were worried that they would be marked by affiliation with their own training analysts and "caught in the crossfire." There was a lack of trust that the analysts would exercise their power over the trainees with fairness and goodwill. There were stories of sexual indiscretions. A candidate or two had managed to "short-circuit" the power differential by becoming physically familiar with an analyst or two, and they as well as others who had rejected sexual overtures were scared of being secretly punished in subsequent evaluations. These and other problems that had not been aired lent an atmosphere of fear and frustration to the yearly convening of the candidate group and to a collective identity as victims of abuse. Child abuse. Incest. Passions of our time. Hence the grumbling.

These are my peers. We suffer together, complain and gossip and laugh together, we cheer each other in our success and console each other in our failure. We also envy the others' successes and are enhanced by their failures as though somehow magically we are thereby more likely to get by—on the shadow side. I guess we feel the same sort of kinship that people feel for one another after they've gone through a long and arduous trial together, such as war or imprisonment or boarding school. In our group, however, the successful ones leave to become analysts, their candidacy at an end. Those of us left behind anticipate the time when we can rejoin our friends, by passing "through the gate." If this sounds familiar, reminiscent of what the preacher says about dying and going to heaven, that's because it is, psychologically speaking.

THE ANALYSTS: *The P.T.A.*

They are our teachers, colleagues, judges, adversaries, role models, therapists, mentors, and sometimes friends and even more. No wonder role confusion and role diffusion are rife in the Inter-Regional Society.

There is an analyst who is my colleague who became my friend and later my consultant. Now that I'm a candidate, he is also my teacher and supervisor and sits in the group that evaluates my progress each year. We used to play tennis regularly and enjoyed the fellowship and exercise, but when we competed, unfortunately I usually won. After one of those "victories," he informed me that I would be required to continue taking didactic seminars for yet another year and a half whether or not I passed the upcoming propaedeuticum. (Heretofore passing that "preliminary" exam had marked the end of such requirement.) Sure enough, the regional training committee had made a "new rule," which has so far applied only to me, that "all candidates" regardless of status had to take these seminars for four years. Now, I'm not objecting to the rule— personally I think it makes good sense. But the timing of its communication to me by this particular messenger makes good sense in quite a different way; a way that illustrates to us the complexity inherent in multiple role relationships. That is to say, this example suggests that the principle of psychological compensation may have acted by discharging through one role set (analyst-candidate) to correct an imbalance created in another role set (court opponents), and vice versa. After this event, I had the feeling I had gotten what I deserved, but only now, much later, can I offer that explanatory hypothesis. We're still friends of course, but we did stop playing tennis together shortly thereafter and now look for less competitive ways to be together. In the Society, a slight stiffness comes up between us because, whereas on the outside we're equals, on the inside we're analyst and candidate. Respecting those complementary roles and the distance and boundary required by them seems both artificial and necessary in the context of my apprenticeship. It will be a lot easier when I'm no longer a candidate.

I'd like to say a word about personal analysis and candidacy—talk about mixing oil and water in a leaky bucket. Candidates are required to be in analysis during the entire term of their training. It's essential to have help in dealing with all the material stirred in the psyche by the training experience. The problem, if you are a candidate, is that your analyst-therapist is a member of the Society and you're not, but you are wishing and hoping and learning to be. Remember the circles and the ones who have the votes. Now, your analyst isn't supposed to (some say isn't required to) participate in the evaluations of your candidacy, and the analyst does leave the room when you are being interviewed or discussed by the group. At meetings, when you see them talking and laughing and going out with their friends who are your examiners, you can't help but wonder what might be passed between them by a word or glance or nuance, whether on purpose or not. Can you keep from trying to make a good impression?

Will you let them see the parts of you you are ashamed of and fairly certain they will dislike? Will they sound the note that dooms you, or will they help you and lay their claim on your success? I think we have here a very sticky situation. Analysts who teach seminars or supervise case conferences are supposed to submit reports on the participants to the regional training committees. What happens when your personal analyst is that teacher or supervisor?

At the Ghost Ranch Conference for Jungian Analysts and Candidates, held annually in New Mexico, someone described the milieu of the analytic society as one in which everyone knows things about everyone else that they have no business knowing, and that's just one of the things we have to learn to deal with. How's that for closeness?

EXAMS: *"Who knows what evil lurks . . ."*

Candidacy, the whole event, from application to graduation or failure, is one long, continual examination. Every contact with an analyst carries the element of judgment, the potential for creating a lasting impression in the mind of the arbiter of the candidate's ultimate fitness for membership. Analysts observe and comment to each other how candidates dress and act at parties, how we come across in meetings and even casual social encounters, not to mention all the formal and informal training functions that generate impressions and reports of our "progress." Grist for the mill.

We are afraid of exams. We see our friends failing their final exams after years of preparation. We see our classmates ("brothers and sisters") terminated from the training program, being told they don't have what it takes to be an analyst, after being told they did have what it takes by virtue of their acceptance into candidacy. Did they lose "it"? If they don't understand or accept their rejection, it is "because" the problem, the fatal flaw, is in their unconscious and by definition they wouldn't be unable to see it the way the analysts can. But who sees the analysts' unconscious?

The only way I can see to survive this ordeal of unrelenting scrutiny is to let go of wanting to win my way into the little circle of those closest to the spirit of C. G. Jung, to trust the outcome of candidacy to the Fates—the circle will open in due time or not at all (all the while, keeping one foot in the ordinary outside world)—and, of course, to do the work. Just be yourself, and if your self is a Jungian analyst then, by gosh, you'll become one, I tell myself.

OTHERS: *Life on the Outside*

Thank goodness for the friends and family and others who keep their distance from "those Jungians" and don't quite understand what I'm doing there with them, and thank goodness for the part of me that doesn't understand. They give me balance. And I can bring them something of what I've gotten from this candidacy, this dancing in the "circle in between."

One of the most important outside contacts in this regard is my work in the university setting. There, with the perfunctory title of Clinical Assistant Professor, I have been teaching a seminar on Jungian psychology for psychiatric residents, and supervising some of them with their patients in individual psychotherapy. These young physicians do not care that I am "only" a candidate. They have more important concerns. Trained mostly in biological medicine, they are hungry for insight and practical advice on how to talk to the people they must treat. No one else tells them about the wounded healer or Eros or the soul, giving words and images for what they know. There, and in my own practice, finding application of what I am learning and seeing the results, I am most acutely aware of the value of the candidates' closeness to the spirit of Jung and to the analytic community that follows him and furthers his teaching.

At the fall 1989 "Closeness" conference in Salado, a group of "outsiders" were invited to attend the lectures and some of the social gatherings. Their presence brought an intrusion into the Jungian concentration and the realization that the Inter-Regional Society exists in fact in a matrix of society at large, and raised consciousness of a need to recognize, define, and accept the place of our Jungian circles in the wider world. Here the concept of closeness finds a collective application for us and our individual integrity as a group is sacrificed.

AFTERTHOUGHTS

This has been a little foray into analytic candidacy reflected to you through one man's experience. I have told you about myself and two of my friends who have helped me along the way. I opened a door, and now would find a way to close it.

It's that way with closeness, isn't it? We get close and maybe even touch, and then we back away. Or we get closer and closer until we collide or pass by or go on through. An old biology professor said that the simplest definition of life is motion. As we move, we get closer to some things and further from others. If we get stuck together in the closeness that closes, we are symbiotic and assumed, and if we get stuck apart, we starve. Being close to the Jungian analytic community as a candidate has been at times like rubbing up against Schopenhauer's porcupine (See Harry Wilmer's Introduction), but in so doing, we are finding our own quills. This closeness separates us candidates from friends and family and ordinary things of everyday life, but it gives up something precious too for us to bring back into that wider world when we return, everyday. Isn't that nice.

The Supervisor

~%~

Joseph Wakefield

This chapter explores issues of closeness in the super-visor-candidate relationship. The thesis is that close-ness between supervisor and candidate is problematic because of the power differential between them: that is, the supervisor has the power to influence the outcome of the candidate's training. Closeness becomes destructive if either the candidate or the supervisor, in a conscious or unconscious way, treats the other as an extension of his or her own needs rather than as a separate person. Closeness is constructive if the roles of supervisor and candidate are recognized and protected. The tasks of supervision include training, assessment and judgment, being a role model, and apprenticeship. I will raise the question of whether closeness between supervisor and candidate should be limited to their specific roles, and whether an "I-Thou" relationship between two whole people is possible.

This chapter should be read on two levels, literal and symbolic.[1]

The first level of understanding is that of literal, historical narrative. On this level, certain errors I made as supervisor are described along with the reasons for those errors. Next I discuss how similar problems afflict others in training programs. This section interprets the problems within transference-countertransference and role theory model. The chapter concludes with specific suggestions as to how supervisors and candidates can overcome the problems described. If one reads on this level alone, one risks personalizing the issues in a reductive way.

The second level of understanding is that of metaphor. Instead of reading my account as describing literal problems requiring concrete solutions, the reader may elect to read it as a teaching story, a fable, or even a timeless mythical event. Read in this manner, the account could be amplified with other archetypal material to broaden its meaning. For example, it could be compared with tales of the shaman or wounded healer who learns from his own wounding and brings this knowledge back to his community. If one reads on this level alone, one risks inflating the account with archetypal grandiosity.

Personal Experiences as Supervisor. Two years ago, I thought I knew what the relationship should be between supervisor and candidate from my experiences as student, intern, resident, and candidate. My most admired role models gave of themselves openly, sharing their doubts and failings as well as their clinical skills. I had twenty years of experience as a supervisor working with medical students, mental health paraprofessionals, psychologists, psychiatrists, and analytic candidates as supervisees.

My first responsibility was to supervise. I encouraged the supervisees to report not only what their patients did, but also to be open about their own experiences as therapists. Countertransference for me was not the narrow issue of unresolved personal complexes, but rather the broad and useful reaction of therapist to patient that let the therapist know what was really happening. I would tell the supervisees, "The surgeon has his operating theater; the radiologist has his X-ray machine; and we have our own psyches. The way we know our psyches in relation to our

patients is through attention to our countertransferences."
When supervisees would report mistakes or actions taken
from their unconscious complexes, I would urge them not
to be too hard on themselves, suggesting, "Your 'mistake'
is an opportunity. What does it teach you about your
patient as well as about yourself? Some mistakes are
inevitable, brought on by what the patient stirs in us, an
unconscious effort to let us know the patient."

To encourage candidates to speak openly about their
countertransference reactions to their patients, I emphasized that they could learn from countertransference, playing down the judging of shortcomings in the candidates'
performances. I preferred to inspire their enthusiasm; let
others pass the heavy hand of judgment upon them! I
ignored the apparent structural contradiction that exists in
the supervisor-candidate relationship: on the one hand, the
call for openness, self-disclosure, and revelation of mistakes; on the other hand, the supervisor as gatekeeper,
capable of judging and failing the candidate.

Since I perceived myself as a role model who encouraged openness and self-disclosure, personal closeness between myself and the trainees followed in an apparently
logical way. On some level, I was aware of the risks of
exploitation of sexualization of the relationships. To avoid
such exploitation, social contacts with the candidates were
made as a group rather than individually. My wife joined
me in such contacts. The informal give and take, the
development of friendships, felt gratifying in a way that
did not stir doubts.

The Shadow Side of Closeness in Supervision. As a junior
member of the training faculty, peripheral to decisions
regarding pass or fail, it was possible to be a supportive
supervisor uninvolved in the hard determinations of the
trainees' adequacy. Over the years, circumstances

changed. The peripheral status grew to one of a senior training analyst who sat upon both admission and evaluation committees, participating in decisions to delay advancement or even dismiss candidates from training. I had become a guardian of the threshold.

Awareness of what my changed status meant to the candidates came painfully. I had been combining required training sessions with social gatherings where my wife and I would entertain the candidate group. Eventually, the candidates confronted me with the meaning of what I had been doing. They suggested that by combining social closeness with a required seminar, the candidates had no opportunity to decline. Since I was a judge and would report to evaluating committees what I saw, the social setting was dangerous for the candidates. Owing to the power differential (my having the power to pass or fail), the candidates could neither give free consent to social closeness, nor could they safely decline without fear of reprisal from me.

My reaction to the candidates' confrontation was one of confusion and then shame. At first I tried to explain what had happened in terms of their psychopathology, but upon reflection, it was obvious that they were right. In other arenas, I was well aware of the uses and abuses of power, so how could I have been blind? This initial defensiveness suggested a guilty conscience. My shadow had been exposed, and I was angry.

In retrospect, how could it have been otherwise? Identification had been entirely with the nurturing, supportive aspect of the supervisor, leaving the judging exerciser of power in the unconscious. Had I not read enough of Jung to know that if the shadow remains unconscious, it can possess us until someone or something forces us to look in the mirror? The conclusion was obvious: unconsciously, I had been using the candidates to meet certain emotional needs, while ignoring their needs for a safe, nonintrusive supervisory experience. To understand this, I returned to personal analysis.

Difficulties of Others with Closeness in Supervision. If these experiences applied only to me, they would be of little importance beyond being one more example of how our unconscious shadow side is an ever-present danger. What happened next makes this chapter of more general interest. To put this experience into context, I inquired if anyone else had had similar problems. Other analysts and the candidates responded quickly. Our analytic society had about ninety members. An informal survey showed that about one-third of them were rumored to have been involved in inappropriate closeness with candidates. Some analysts were rumored to have had sexual relationships with candidates. Male analysts predominated over female analysts in these rumors by a four-to-one margin. Some analysts were rumored to involve the candidates in social relationships in a way that made objective assessment impossible, while others were rumored to coerce candidates into the analyst's "school" or theoretical opinion in a way that blocked the candidates' freedom to define themselves. The results of these behaviors were grim. Of the twenty-eight analysts rumored to be problematic, eighteen had withdrawn from participation in clinical teaching. Several withdrew from the society; several remained for contact with colleagues but wanted no further contact with candidates. One of those who withdrew said to me, "Whatever we did was wrong. If we kept our distance in formal seminars, the candidates complained they weren't receiving enough real relatedness. If we combined seminars with group dinners, the candidates complained we were intruding upon their privacy. After a while, I just got tired and gave up." These analysts' experiences represented not only personal disillusionment, but also a great loss of training resources for the society.

Could it be that this analytic society was seething with unconscious exploitation? The next question was how other societies had dealt with such problems. The same guilty confusion appeared everywhere. One coastal society had had to dismiss two prominent training supervisors in a row for sexual involvements with their supervisees. The society membership tried to correct itself by passing a strict code of ethics. An unexpected consequence was that the analysts began refusing to teach or supervise candidates for fear of being accused of inappropriate closeness. Of course, the analysts began avoiding social contact with candidates. The candidates felt abandoned.

In another European society, several senior male analysts were rumored to have involved themselves sexually with candidates. This society elected in an unspoken way not to confront the problem. Instead, an informal network developed between the female analysts and female candidates to warn and protect the candidates against exploitation. It became one of those guilty secrets that everyone knew but no one would discuss out loud.

I turned to the analytic society that had cradled me for comfort, hoping to find an oasis, an organization based on ethical awareness and consideration. Renewal of membership put me on the newsletter mailing list. My discovery was cold comfort indeed. Page after page arrived describing candidates' meetings calling for dismissal of their supervisors, dismissal of their evaluating committees, even suspension of the society's training program. The cause? A disturbing blurring of the supervisor-supervisee boundaries because of inappropriate closeness. The analysts reacted with a mixture of guilt, defensiveness, anger at their colleagues, and at last weariness. The clinic directors wondered why they were unable to find analysts willing to supervise candidates. In their meetings, the analysts debated whether or not the candidates might be right, that perhaps it would be best to suspend the training program.

How had it come about that the supervisor-supervisee relationship, begun with such high hopes, was now rife with mutual distrust and withdrawal?

What Can Be Learned from Others? First, it seemed that the problem was widespread. Concern about closeness and the abuse of power existed in every training society examined. It was obvious that this concern had reached the collective consciousness. Our daily newspaper and the evening television news carried articles about child abuse, especially sexual abuse. Conversations with women colleagues quickly revealed that they were quite familiar with the issue of abuse of power in gender politics. I recalled reading the social protest essays and literature in Central America that contained the recurrent theme of exploitation of the powerless by those in power.

Whenever a cultural mass movement occurs, there is some danger of being swept up in a general hysteria. With regard to child sexual abuse, concern had begun to be expressed about a "witch hunt" atmosphere in which nonpathological forms of closeness could be interpreted as abusive.[2] I wondered if appropriate forms of closeness in the supervisory relationship were being viewed as abusive due to the current atmosphere in our culture.

Of course I was not alone in these reflections. Our analytic training society had begun a process of self-examination that came to focus in the fall 1989 conference on closeness sponsored by Harry Wilmer and the Salado Institute for the Humanities. That conference, with its lectures, small-group discussions, and personal soul-searching, was the stimulus for this book.

The social protest literature and literature on abuse of power in gender politics stirs in us feelings of outrage and a need to change something. We proclaim a moral imperative: we must right an injustice! The most powerful expression of this I know is the theology of liberation proclaimed by Jon Sobrino.[3] The mythic image is of the incarnation of Christ in the meek and powerless. If we stand by and allow those in power to abuse the powerless, we are like Pontius Pilate washing our hands of the crucifixion. A powerful moral imperative indeed!

The literature on child abuse, especially sexual abuse, also stirs among us feelings of outrage, but my personal feelings are more complex and include sadness and a sense of loss. Here is not pure exploitation, but also a longing for love, for closeness, that went dreadfully wrong. Another, less socially acceptable feeling is present—pleasure at the fantasy of dominating another—and I wonder if this feeling's very unacceptability makes it likely to be repressed and then enacted in the shadow. Some dark impulses cannot be spoken in polite society. In Nabokov's *Lolita*, the character Humbert Humbert can admit his pedophilic desire for Lolita only by imagining confessing to a jury that will condemn him.[4] So I wonder what metaphor dominates our thought about the supervisor-candidate relationship? Are supervisors thought of as parents and candidates as children? Is sexuality between supervisor and candidate a form of incest? If so, the horror and fascination of the totally forbidden will be present. If so, then, as Jung has taught us in "The Psychology of the Transference," the participants in the drama will be in the grip of a desire to know and be known by the Self.[5]

The very terms *abuse, exploitation,* and *power* stir feelings. Something is being denied. Adolf Guggenbühl-Craig, in *Power in the Helping Professions*, contrasts power and Eros.[6] Power without Eros leads to evil, destructiveness, abuse, and failure. Well, then, the supervisor-candidate relationship needs Eros! But what does "love" mean in that specific context? Are we thinking of supervisor-candidate the way we think of analyst-analysand? Again, this raises the structural contradiction in the supervisor-candidate relationship: on the one hand, openness, self-disclosure, and revelation, just as an analyst would encourage his analysand; on the other hand, the supervisor as a judge. How can the candidate reveal himself if he risks condemnation? Suppose the supervisor finds the candidate not ready, or even not capable? Suppose the supervisor in his judgment calls for that candidate's dismissal? Are power and Eros mutually exclusive? Can a supervisor be informed by Eros even as the candidate experiences the supervisor's judgment as rejection?

A theme emerges for me from Goffman's *Asylums*,[7] which I read thirty years ago, and Karl Weick's lucid description given at the "Closeness' conference (see page 181): what people do within organizations can be understood in terms of the social roles they are called upon to perform. A society (including an analytic training society) can become dysfunctional when conflicting, incongruent roles are in force. So the contradiction in the supervisor-candidate relationship could be understood in terms of role theory: the role of supervisor as nurturer, stimulator, role model for the candidate, and the role of supervisor as judge and gatekeeper for the candidate. In such a system, the candidates would long for greater social intimacy with the supervisor to obtain the role modeling needed for their apprenticeship and at the same time, they would be apprehensive of social intimacy with the supervisor for fear of being judged and rejected.

Role theory stirs an odd reaction within me: admiration for its clarity of thought, the explanations that in retrospect seem so obvious. What a relief to set aside moralizing, blaming individuals, and using psychopathological terms to explain dysfunction within a society. For me, reading role theory is like walking on a cold, dark mountain trail and coming to a way station that is well lit, warm, and nourishing. Ah, what pleasure to enter a world where rational thought holds sway! Yet I cannot stay. What dark force compels me to go out again into the wilderness in an effort to bring the individual, the irrational, and the unconscious into the equation? I had turned to Carl Jung's psychology twenty-five years before because rational, conscious explanations were not enough. To explain "disorder," be it individual or group, I feel the need to ask, "What purpose is being served? What are psyche, soul, the Self trying to do? How can we integrate this shadow side of closeness in supervision?"

Peter Rutter's *Sex in the Forbidden Zone* had an enormous impact on the analytic community when it appeared in 1989.[8] Subtitled *When Men in Power—Therapists, Doctors, Clergy, Teachers, and Others—Betray Women's Trust,* this book speaks eloquently. A problem that had been whispered about among analysts now was out in the open: the exploitation of relationships of inequality for sexual gratification. Rutter not only describes what happens and its consequences, but tries to show why it happens. To the content of this book, I can only say, "Amen." The feeling tone of the book gives me pause. As with the social protest literature from Latin America, it seems to present a passionate call to correct injustice. What metaphor speaks to us here? Do we experience the supervisor-candidate dyad as oppressor-oppressed? In the supervisor do we imagine Uranus-Cronus-father-rapist, devourer of his own children, needing to be castrated by his own sickle? Are problems with relationships of unequal power limited to sexuality?

Many of the candidates have contributed to what is written here. In small-group and individual discussions, we struggle to sort out what were the appropriate parameters of our relationships. Beyond "appropriate," we struggled to understand the forces that moved us.

The central question is: what are the problems and the opportunities in the supervisor-candidate relationship?

Transference and Countertransference in Supervision. How may the unconscious enter into the work between supervisor and candidate? How may we use or misuse what is offered? Transference and countertransference are spoken of here as they apply to the supervisor-candidate relationship.

Among other dimensions of the supervisor-candidate relationship exists the dimension of transference projections. By definition, these projections are, at least at first, unconscious. Supervisors trained as analysts try to recognize transference projections when they occur in therapy. Boundaries of the therapist-patient relationship are to be maintained; the rule of abstinence is to be followed; and efforts are to be made to analyze the transference (that is, bring the projections into awareness so that here-and-now experiences can be linked with similar reactions to others in the past). Jungian analysts would add the dimension of linking the here-and-now projections onto the analyst with the patient's self, both personal and archetypal. We try to know what they are about when such projections occur in therapy. Ah, but the supervisor-candidate relationship is *not* therapy! We have agreed to supervise, not to analyze,

projections. Should supervisors note transference projections coming toward them, many will advise candidates to
explore them with their personal analyst rather than discuss them in supervision. Historically, the boundaries of
the supervisor-candidate relationship have been less clearly
defined than those of therapist-patient. The combination
of unanalyzed projections and unclear boundaries is a
prescription for enactment of the projections in that the
persons involved take their impressions of the other and
their feelings as literally true, at which point it seems
natural to make their feelings concrete by acting upon
them.

Then we have countertransference. Again, members of
analytic societies aspire to know something about countertransference when they are engaged in therapy. With
countertransference in therapy, we try once more to maintain boundaries, abstain, and make the unconscious projections conscious. The mandate is less clear in the supervisor-candidate relationship though we are evolving toward
such awareness as the closeness conference and this book
indicate. Therapist and patient have stronger barriers
against acting out unconscious projections than do supervisor and candidate.

As I reread the previous paragraphs on the response to
transference, I worry about their sounding punitive.
Boundaries, abstinence, and analyzing projections: Ugh!
Not much fun there! So it is worthwhile to remember why
we abstain and why we analyze. It is precisely here where
archetypal psychology, classical Jungian psychology, and
psychoanalysis agree. Archetypal psychologists such as
James Hillman urge us not to make experience literal and
concrete experience, for "soul-making" with psyche requires the play of metaphor.

In his essay "Observations on Transference Love"

(1915), Freud describes how it is possible to work through eroticized transference by remaining within the analytic container. He acknowledges the temptation to act upon feelings, then states:

> And yet the analyst is absolutely debarred from giving way. However highly he may prize love, he must prize even more highly the opportunity to help his patient over a decisive moment in her life. . . . To achieve this mystery of herself, she must be taken through the primordial era of her mental development and in this way reach that greater freedom within the mind which distinguishes conscious mental activity—in the systematic sense—from unconsciousness.[9]

In his essay "The Psychology of the Transference," Jung utilized imagery from alchemy to elucidate the intense urge toward unconscious merger and transformation that occurs with an erotic transference and countertransference. He describes the man projecting his anima and the woman her animus upon the other, and he warns of the danger of taking the projection too literally.

> It is a mistake to believe that one's personal dealings with one's partner play the most important part. Quite the reverse: the most important part falls to the man's dealings with the anima and the woman's dealings with the animus. . . . Although the two figures are always tempting the ego to identify with them, a real understanding even on the personal level is possible only if the identification is refused. Nonidentification demands considerable moral effort. . . . The personal protagonists in the royal game should constantly bear in mind that at bottom, it represents the "trans-subjective" union of archetypal figures, and it should never be forgotten that it is a *symbolical* relationship whose goal is complete individuation.[10]

What sort of projections may occur between supervisor and candidate? My examples will be expressed within three main currents of contemporary psychoanalytic metapsychology: drive theory, object relations theory, and the self psychology of Heinz Kohut.[11] I shall use the different theories as frameworks for describing the kind of projections that can occur.

Drives. The primordial instincts are Eros and Thanatos, sex and power. Within this context, either supervisor or candidate could experience the other as a source of gratification of instinctual desire. Yet the world is filled with potential sources of gratification, so why select precisely one that is forbidden? Sex becomes power and power becomes sex: a supervisor engaged in a sexual relationship with a candidate might not dare give a negative judgment to that candidate, and a candidate wanting to pass might not dare to turn down a sexual overture from a supervisor.

Power may express itself in nonsexual forms, of course. Suppose the supervisor wishes to dominate or control the candidate, insisting that the candidate adopt the supervisor's point of view. If so, the candidate might feel that he or she must submit in order to graduate, either in case supervision, writing a thesis, or oral exams. In a subtle, corrupt way, the candidate might select a power-driven analyst as supervisor precisely to neutralize that analyst through flattery. The candidate may well be conscious of the analyst's unconscious needs, but feel that he or she must not dare say anything for fear of retribution.

Object Relations. The focus shifts from instinctual gratification to the importance of relationships, especially relationships early in development. In terms of analytical psychology, we enter the world of complexes, including parental complexes and sibling relationships. Either supervisor or candidate may project upon the other certain of their complexes. For candidates, supervisors may represent the caring, guiding parents they never had, or the cruel, withholding parents, or even the possibility of achieving an Oedipal triumph at last by becoming the favorite child, intensely if secretly loved. For supervisors, candidates may represent the child they lost or the child they never had or the child in themselves whom they wish to nourish the way they wished they had been nourished.

Neither gender nor age limit the transferential projections that the complexes can unleash. I recall being the analyst of a woman several years younger than myself. As we sorted out her transference projections (and I worked upon my countertransference), we discovered multiple coexisting projections. At various times, sometimes in the same session, she experienced me as father, as mother, as sibling, as her child, as her lover, as an all-powerful magician (either benevolent or malevolent), and as a fool. For my part, I found that she stirred impulses to protect, a desire to rock her on my lap and sing a lullaby, sexual desire, impulses to pronounce the Word as authority, a longing for her to mother me, and often enough I felt foolish. All of this is normal, everyday experience of transference and countertransference within analysis. All that I have described can occur between supervisor and candidate as well. It is because of such projections that in analysis we have boundaries, the rule of abstinence, and efforts to analyze projections.

Projection of complexes may occur not only between supervisor and candidate. The candidate may be caught in sibling rivalries that can exist between analysts. Consider the analyst who wants to be "top dog," who expresses his or her envy and competitiveness with other analysts by attacking the candidates who are in analysis or supervision with other analysts. Of course, the expression of this may be subtle. The competitive analyst may say he or she is trying to help the candidate by pointing out "blind spots" that the candidate's personal analyst has. The competitive analyst may even suggest the candidate would benefit by changing personal analysts or supervisors to avoid such blind spots and broaden the candidate's experience. To survive, the candidate may be aware of the analyst's unconscious needs but may fear the consequences of saying anything.

Self Psychology. A subset of complexes, the narcissistic complexes, has been of great interest to analysts in recent years. Heinz Kohut has developed his own vocabulary and his own school of followers in exploring these complexes. For the purpose of this chapter, I find useful his description of three types of narcissistic transference.

In the idealizing transference, the person projects ideals onto the other and expects the other to live up to the projection. In terms of analytical psychology, we could say that some aspects of the Self have been projected, perhaps as the Hero or as the Wise Old Man or Woman. If the other fails to live up to the projection (as eventually happens, for all of us are human, all too human), the idealization quickly turns into denigration and rage. Either the supervisor or the candidate may project an idealizing transference onto the other. Since it feels good to be viewed as wise, good, and heroic, the recipient of the projection may question nothing. These situations may lead to the candidate's overvaluing the supervisor, loss of the ability to see weaknesses and shortcomings, and a type of enslavement in which the candidate blindly follows his or her ideal while attacking analysts who have different points of view. I suspect that it is from such unanalyzed transferences that psychoanalytic "schools" based upon the Great Founder surrounded by devoted disciples have evolved.

In the mirror of transference (or self-object transference), the projector expects the recipient of the projection to mirror back what the projector wants to see of himself or herself. The projector wants to be idealized and may become enraged if this is not done. Either supervisor or candidate may project such a transference upon the other. The supervisor may expect the candidate to be a mute witness of the supervisor's brilliance and skill. Conversely, the candidate may expect the supervisor to say nothing while listening in silent awe to the superb presentations of the candidate. As you may expect, efforts to correct shortcomings may be met with resentment.

In the twinship transference (or alter ego transference), the projector wishes the other to be a double of himself or herself. Again, such projections may occur between supervisor and candidate. Consider the supervisor who acts as if "we are all equal," as if no power differential or gatekeeper function exists. Such a supervisor might view candidates as his peers, as his friends, as his confidants. A candidate might treat his supervisors similarly. While it is true on a level of basic humanity that we are all equal, it is illusory to have such a belief about supervisor and candidate. Built into the very role each has in relation to the other is an inequality, a difference. To ignore such differences is to blind themselves to the reality of what each is required to do for the other.

A final observation regarding transference projections between supervisor and candidate: while such projections exist and remain unconscious, closeness is problematic. The projector may feel love, rage, desire, or awe toward the recipient of the projection. Sadly, the actual other person is not known as he or she really is. As Elie Humbert describes it, the projector is "in pursuit of his own desire." With such projections intact, empathy toward the actual other cannot occur, and the other is known as an extension of the projector's needs rather than as a separate person in his or her own right.

The Emotional Impact of Supervision upon the Supervisors. Upon realizing that I had been intruding upon the candidates, my first impulse was to offer to resign from supervision. Since the informal survey of my training society revealed that eighteen of twenty-eight analysts rumored to be "too close" had withdrawn from teaching, I imagine the impulse to withdraw is common. Under the best of circumstances, supervision is hard work: teaching for a fraction of customary analytic fees, meeting candidates in evenings or on weekends to accommodate their schedules, being the target of anger from candidates and some analysts if the candidate is judged not ready to advance. Then there is the possibility of being the target of negative transference projections from the candidate that may be acted out in some unpleasant way. When my own failings were added to the list, it seemed to much! After due reflection, however, I concluded that supervision is not only possible but very much worthwhile. There are non-relationship reasons to engage in supervision:

Supervision educates the supervisor as well as the candidate. The preparation time, uncompensated financially, is a rich source of learning for the supervisor. Supervisors learn from the candidates, both theory and clinical skills.

Supervision is a form of community service. Serving on committees or participating in teaching is part of what it can mean to be professional, where the analyst serves the profession as well as patients and himself or herself.

Supervision is compensated financially. There are community standards for acceptable fees for supervision and teaching. If either supervisor or candidate tries to depart from such standards, I would see a signal. If the supervisor doesn't want to receive money, what does the supervisor want? Gratitude is too high a price to pay.

Supervision brings the supervisor into a community of peers, other supervisors, with whom he or she can share experiences and provide mutual support. The supervisor need not be alone.

I come to the question that opened this chapter. What sort of closeness should take place between supervisor and candidate?

Closeness, Intimacy, and Empathy in Supervision. The discovery that I had intruded upon the candidates unconsciously stirred a profound sadness within me. I remembered the admonition of Hippocrates: *Primum non nocere*, the first duty of a physician is to do no harm. Such intrusions could not continue. Unfortunately, the alternative seemed to be a withdrawal of myself as a person from the supervisor-candidate relationship. It seemed I could not be present as a whole person but only as a part-object. While this conclusion seemed logical, it felt dreadfully wrong. Jungian analytic candidate James Shultz helped me out of this conceptual blind alley by giving me a recording of a talk by Douglas Ingram titled "Legitimate Intimacy in Analytic Therapy."[12] While Ingram's focus is on analytic therapy, much of his thought is applicable to the supervision relationship.

Ingram defines intimacy in both experiential and transactional terms. As an experience, intimacy occurs when one's authentic self is engaged. As a transaction, intimacy occurs when one's authentic self is engaged with another in a comprehensible way.

Intimacy is understood within social role theory, and Ingram defines roles as goal-directed configurations of transactions between people within a social context. Roles mediate the interaction of oneself with the self of another. Just as roles have limits and boundaries, intimacy also has limits and boundaries. Intimacy exists within the possible limits of the role system. It is in appreciating the limits that intimacy itself is enhanced. Intimacy accepts the role system and is inseparable from it. Intimacy connects the self of one with the self of another within a social role system.

The character of intimacy between persons changes as their role relationships change.

Ingram describes three functions of intimacy. First, it enables a reduction of defenses that restricts the unity of the personal self within a social context. Thus, intimate relationships can contribute toward self-realization and growth. Second, intimacy facilitates engaging oneself with another, conveying meaning beyond the personal self. Third, intimacy confirms the role system in which it arises.

Pathology may occur when current relationships are burdened by attempts to overcome deficiencies in intimacy that occurred in earlier relationships. If one or both persons attempt to blur the social roles and overstep limits, there may be a loss of intimacy. Ingram describes this blurring of roles as familiarity. For example, this may occur in therapy with an erotic transference where the projector seeks fusion and merger in a closeness that "knows no bounds." If the projection is enacted, there is a blurring of the roles of therapist and patient and with it a loss of the intimacy that belongs to the therapist-patient roles.

Only in intimacy-valued relationships can empathy occur. Empathy involves the self of one engaging the self of another. Such engagement can take place only where respect for the role structure allows intimacy to develop.

A "real" relationship between two "whole persons," which is intimate, develops when each relates to the other authentically, in a trustworthy manner, within the context of their social roles. For example, an analysand can experience his or her analyst as a whole, authentic self as long as the vehicle, the analysis, remains intact.

Consider the question of closeness within supervision from Ingram's viewpoint. Some forms of closeness, such as familiarity, may actually destroy intimacy because they undermine the social roles required of supervisor and candidate. Other forms of closeness may enhance intimacy and therefore contribute to an authentic connection of self between the persons involved.

Peter Rutter and Douglas Ingram both describe erotic transference as seeking fusion, merger, and the setting aside of boundaries. By its nature, an erotic transference tends to weaken established roles within a supervisory relationship. I agree with what they have said, but would not limit problematic closeness to erotic transference and sexual enactment. I have described a variety of transference projections that can undermine the relationship. These transferences include Eros, power, complexes from early life relationships, and narcissistic complexes. The uniting principle is that such projections blind the projector to the reality of the other in an effort to turn the other into an extension of the projector's needs.

What should be done when transference projections arise between supervisor and candidate? Supervision is not analysis. No agreement exists for either the supervisor or the candidate to interpret the other's projections. At the least, they should agree not to interpret literally and concretely enact feelings that would cause them to depart from their roles of supervisor and supervisee, trying to make conscious the meaning of their feelings by discussing them with their personal analyst or with a colleague.

When both supervisor and candidate perform their roles, over time and in a trustworthy manner, intimacy may develop between them. This intimacy is the expression of relatedness between the authentic selves of each person involved. This is legitimate closeness within the supervisor-candidate relationship. Viewed in this way, the apparent structural contradiction in the role of supervisor dissolves. The role of gatekeeper and the role of nurturing role model are not opposed. The role of supervisor includes both gatekeeper (guardian of the community) and mentor of the candidate.

Under the mutual, respectful performance of the roles of supervisor and candidate, intimacy and the authentic relatedness can evolve in the mutual exploration of what Carl Jung called "doctor of the soul."[13]

NOTES

1. Paul Kugler, "Childhood Seduction: Physical and Emotional," *Spring* (1987), pp. 40–60; James Hillman, "A Psychology of Transgression Drawn from an Incest Dream," *Spring* (1987), pp. 66–76.

2. See Hollida Wakefield, ed., *Issues in Child Abuse Accusations*, Winter 1990.

3. Jon Sobrino, "Compañeros de Jesus: El asesinato martirio de los jesuitas Salvadoreños," in *Eca: Estudios Centroamericanos* 493–494 (November–December 1989): 1041–1074.

4. Vladimir Nabokov, *Lolita* (New York: Perigee Books, Putnam Publishing Group, 1972).

5. C. G. Jung, "The Psychology of the Transference" (1946), in *The Practice of Psychotherapy, Collected Works* 16 (Princeton, N.J.: Princeton University Press, 1966), pp. 163–323.

6. Adolf Guggenbühl-Craig, *Power in the Helping Professions* (Dallas: Spring Publications, 1971).

7. Irving Goffman, *Asylums: Essays on the Social Situation of Mental Patients and Other Inmates* (New York: Doubleday/Anchor Books, 1961).

8. Peter Rutter, *Sex in the Forbidden Zone: When Men in Power—Therapists, Doctors, Clergy, Teachers, and Others—Betray Women's Trust* (Los Angeles: Jeremy P. Tarcher, 1989).

9. Sigmund Freud, "Observations on Transference Love" (1915), in *Therapy and Technique*, ed. Philip Rieff (New York: Collier Books, 1963) pp. 178–179.

10. Jung, "The Psychology of the Transference," para. 469.

11. An excellent review can be found in Jay Greenberg and Stephen Mitchell, *Object Relations in Psychoanalytic Theory* (Cambridge: Harvard University Press, 1983).

12. Douglas Ingram, "Legitimate Intimacy in Analytic Therapy," panel discussion on erotic transference and countertransference, given at the 33rd annual meeting of the American Academy of Psychoanalysis, San Francisco, May 1989.

13. Jung, "The Shadow" (1948), in *Aion, CW* 9, part 2 (Princeton, N.J.: Princeton University Press, 1959), pp. 9–10.

Separation

A Poem by Harry A. Wilmer

I told him a dream and he said nothing.
So I told him what it meant.
All he said was,
YOU HAVE IT!
YOU HAVE IT!

What do you think, I asked. You're right.
  Exactly right.
  You see it.
  YOU HAVE IT.

          Inner thought: What a disappointment!
          I was shocked to have it all by myself,
          knowing the conundrum paradox,
          unobfuscating a dream
          in the light of my own truth.

It was so clear to me, really.
Crystal clear.
Simple clear.
I rejoiced.

Inner thought:
What a disappointment! Goddamnit!
That blows it.
What's more,
I don't want to hear what
I want him to say.

The Wise Old One didn't say it anyway.
I heard myself say it.
I knew I had it.
Even if I didn't want it.
I treasure it,
the treasure hard to find.

For years, we have been psychologically near to each
    other.

Now I knew what
had been germinating, gestating inside me
all the time. Bright and shining and smiling,
it had come to term
not termination.

Muse! Muse! Musing to myself. I look around:
Where did the awesome, shining Wise Old One go?
He is nowhere to be seen or heard,
leaving myself to my Self.

Now I know,
Stumbling, spontaneous, naively wise,
just right: I have it:
Given by the Wise Old One
because I took it.
In several ways to look at it, I took it
And in the end, nourished, contented,
at the ending was the beginning.

Other C. G. Jung Foundation Books from Shambhala Publications

Absent Fathers, Lost Sons: The Search for Masculine Identity, by Guy Corneau.

★*The Child*, by Erich Neumann. Foreword by Louis H. Stewart.

Cross-Currents of Jungian Thought: An Annotated Bibliography, by Donald R. Dyer.

★*Depth Psychology and a New Ethic*, by Erich Neumann. Forewords by C. G. Jung, Gerhard Adler, and James Yandell.

★*Dreams*, by Marie-Louise von Franz.

★*From Freud to Jung: A Comparative Study of the Psychology of the Unconscious*, by Liliane Frey-Rohn. Foreword by Robert Hinshaw.

A Guided Tour of the Collected Works *of C. G. Jung*, by Robert H. Hopcke. Foreword by Aryeh Maidenbaum.

Individuation in Fairy Tales, Revised Edition, by Marie-Louise von Franz.

In Her Image: The Unhealed Daughter's Search for Her Mother, by Kathie Carlson.

★*The Inner Child in Dreams*, by Kathrin Asper.

Knowing Woman: A Feminine Psychology, by Irene Claremont de Castillejo.

Lingering Shadows: Jungians, Freudians, and Anti-Semitism, edited by Aryeh Maidenbaum and Stephen A. Martin.

The Old Wise Woman: A Study of Active Imagination, by Rix Weaver. Introduction by C. A. Meier.

Power and Politics: The Psychology of Soviet-American Partnership, by Jerome S. Bernstein. Forewords by Senator Claiborne Pell and Edward C. Whitmont, M.D.

Continued on next page

The Way of All Women, by M. Esther Harding. Introduction by C. G. Jung.

The Wisdom of the Dream: The World of C. G. Jung, by Stephen Segaller and Merrill Berger.

Woman's Mysteries: Ancient and Modern, by M. Esther Harding. Introduction by C. G. Jung.

★Published in association with Daimon Verlag, Einsiedeln, Switzerland.